P9-DXT-813

NEW DIRECTIONS FOR STUDENT SERVICES

John H. Schuh, *Iowa State University*
EDITOR-IN-CHIEF

Elizabeth J. Whitt, *University of Iowa*
ASSOCIATE EDITOR

The Role Student Aid Plays in Enrollment Management

Michael D. Coomes
Bowling Green State University

EDITOR

Number 89, Spring 2000

JOSSEY-BASS PUBLISHERS
San Francisco

THE ROLE STUDENT AID PLAYS IN ENROLLMENT MANAGEMENT
Michael D. Coomes (ed.)
New Directions for Student Services, no. 89
John H. Schuh, Editor-in-Chief
Elizabeth J. Whitt, Associate Editor

Microfilm copies of issues and articles are available in 16mm and 35mm, as well as microfiche in 105mm, through University Microfilms Inc., 300 North Zeeb Road, Ann Arbor, Michigan 48106-1346.

ISSN 0164-7970   ISBN 0-7879-5378-4

NEW DIRECTIONS FOR STUDENT SERVICES is part of The Jossey-Bass Higher and Adult Education Series and is published quarterly by Jossey-Bass Inc., Publishers, 350 Sansome Street, San Francisco, California 94104-1342. Periodicals postage paid at San Francisco, California, and at additional mailing offices. Postmaster: Send address changes to New Directions for Student Services, Jossey-Bass Inc., Publishers, 350 Sansome Street, San Francisco, California 94104-1342.

New Directions for Student Services is indexed in College Student Personnel Abstracts and Contents Pages in Education.

SUBSCRIPTIONS cost $58.00 for individuals and $104.00 for institutions, agencies, and libraries. See ordering information page at end of book.

EDITORIAL CORRESPONDENCE should be sent to the Editor-in-Chief, John H. Schuh, N 243 Lagomarcino Hall, Iowa State University, Ames, Iowa 50011

Cover photograph by Wernher Krutein/PHOTOVAULT © 1990.

Jossey-Bass Web address: www.josseybass.com

Manufactured in the United States of America on acid-free recycled paper containing 100 percent recovered waste paper, of which at least 20 percent is postconsumer waste.

CONTENTS

EDITOR'S NOTES   1
Michael D. Coomes

1. The Historical Roots of Enrollment Management   5
Michael D. Coomes
This chapter examines the development of student aid and enrollment management as a concept and functional area.

2. Federal and State Aid in the 1990s: A Policy Context for   19
Enrollment Management
Shirley A. Ort
The demographic, economic, and social forces of the past decade provide a policy context for examining the purposes of enrollment management.

3. Enrollment Management, Institutional Resources, and the   33
Private College
Joseph A. Russo, Michael D. Coomes
Institutional student aid policies are tied to campus enrollment goals. This chapter examines tuition discounting, student aid packaging policy, and merit scholarships.

4. Alternative Financing Methods for College   47
Robert DeBard
This chapter compares borrowing and work as effective methods for supporting persistence. It discusses suggestions for expanding available means of financing a postsecondary education at the institutional, state, and federal levels.

5. The Impact of Student Aid on Recruitment and Retention: 61
What the Research Indicates
Edward P. St. John
This chapter offers an extensive review of the literature on the relationship of student aid to college choice and student persistence.

6. The Role of Financial Aid in Enrollment Management   77
Don Hossler
Institutional policy and organizational structures can effectively shape enrollment goals. The author offers recommendations for ethical enrollment planning.

7. Recommended Reading   91

Marie T. Saddlemire

This annotated list of resources will be of use to enrollment planners,
researchers, and institutional policymakers.

INDEX   97

EDITOR'S NOTES

The College Board (1998, p. 3) sums it up well:

> For most Americans, college remains accessible, especially with the avail-
> ability of more than $60 billion in financial aid. . . . Combined with stagnant
> family income over the past fifteen years, however, trends in college tuition
> present serious problems for low- and moderate-income families. While aver-
> age, inflation-adjusted tuition has more than doubled at both public and pri-
> vate four-year institutions, median family income has risen only 12 percent
> since 1981. Student aid, meanwhile, has increased in total value, but not
> enough to keep pace with the rise in tuition, and most of the growth has been
> in the form of student borrowing.

Student financial aid has always been burdened by a complex interplay
of institutional needs and public policy goals; that interplay, in the past
twenty years, has been confounded by increasing consumerism on the part
of students and parents. For example, state and federal policymakers have
supported the policy goal of assuring educational opportunity since the
early 1950s. That goal resulted in a set of student aid programs (the
National Defense Student Loan, College Work Study, and Supplemental
Educational Opportunity Grants) and institutional options (such as community colleges) intended to broaden access to postsecondary education. In
the 1970s, the goal of institutional choice was added to access through
increased levels of support for student aid and the creation of new programs
such as the Federal Pell Grant program. In the 1980s, calls for reduced
spending on education, competing funding priorities at the state level, and
concerns about the quality of an undergraduate degree shaped higher education policy. The 1990s have been characterized by rising college costs,
increased consumerism, and use of financial aid to meet both student needs
and campus enrollment goals. It is the purpose of this volume of *New Directions for Student Services* to provide an assessment of the current role that
student financial aid plays in the enrollment management process. I hope
that this volume will provide readers with a better understanding of the
complex interplay of student aid and enrollment management and will be
of help to campus policymakers as they consider student aid and enrollment
policies in the future.

In Chapter One, I offer an overview of the historical development of
enrollment management as a management philosophy and organizational
concept. I pay special attention to the development of a federal system of
student aid programs and the role that student aid has played in advancing

the goals of educational access and choice. I also examine the development of research on the processes of college choice and student persistence.

Building on the first chapter, Shirley A. Ort in Chapter Two provides an additional context for understanding enrollment management. She examines the context of both state and federal policymaking in the 1990s, exploring the relationships of demographic, social, and economic forces to the development of federal and state higher education policy. She concludes with a plea for better informed policy, linked more closely to sound research and targeted at enhanced enrollment practices.

In Chapter Three, Joseph A. Russo and I examine the role that student aid plays in meeting the goals of enrollment management at independent colleges. We pay special attention to the uses of merit scholarships and differential student aid packaging policies, and review recent discussions of college cost. Finally, we explain a new model of delivery for student aid service and examine a range of future issues.

Robert DeBard explores alternative methods for financing a college education in Chapter Four. His comments center on the relationship of student loans to college choice and student persistence issues. After noting a number of arguments against borrowing, he makes a persuasive case for the use of student employment and cooperative education as financing mechanisms. DeBard also provides a discussion of the addition of tuition tax credits and educational savings plans to the student aid puzzle.

The research on the relationship of student aid to college choice and student persistence is summarized by Edward P. St. John in Chapter Five. St. John begins his discussion by exploring both theoretical and methodological challenges to studying the impact of student aid on college choice and student persistence. That discussion is followed by a meta-analysis of the research on the impact of student aid on recruitment and retention.

Chapter Six, by Don Hossler, presents the views of an acknowledged expert on the theory and practice of enrollment management. Drawing on his experiences as a scholar and campus enrollment manager, Hossler summarizes the purposes of enrollment management and student financial aid. He pays particular attention to the role that student aid plays in the process of college choice. Hossler also outlines a series of steps that campuses can follow to link administrative processes more effectively between the offices of financial aid and admissions. He concludes with a discussion of ethical issues that campus policymakers must confront as they continue to integrate student aid with the enrollment and retention process.

The volume concludes with Marie T. Saddlemire's annotated bibliography of resources on student financial aid and enrollment management. Topics include enrollment management foundations, strategies and structures for implementing enrollment management, recent research on student aid trends, and the link between financial aid and enrollment management. Electronic media are discussed, as well as traditional printed resources.

Michael D. Coomes
Editor

Reference

College Board. *Trends in College Pricing, 1998.* Washington, D.C.: College Board, 1998.

MICHAEL D. COOMES *is associate professor of higher education and student affairs and chair of the college student personnel program at Bowling Green State University.*

1

This chapter examines the historical development of enrollment management. It focuses on the roles that federal student aid legislation, changing student demographics, and research on college impact have played in shaping enrollment management as a concept.

The Historical Roots of Enrollment Management

Michael D. Coomes

Since the early 1970s, enrollment management has become an increasingly important function for colleges. That function grew out of the traditional gatekeeper role of the admissions officer (Hossler, 1996), and in recent years has been linked with student aid in an effort to attract students and retain them in college. Governmental policymakers, college administrators, students, and their families all recognize that student aid plays an important role in assisting both students and institutions in meeting their enrollment goals. In this chapter, I will provide a context for understanding the emergence of enrollment management on campus. My primary focus will be on the confluence of three late-twentieth-century events: the emergence of generally available student aid resources (primarily through federally funded programs), the development of an extensive college impact literature, and changes in the organizational structures of universities.

Pre-Twentieth-Century Conditions

As is the case with much of postsecondary education, it all began with Harvard College. Seven years after its founding, Lady Ann Radcliff Mowlson bequeathed to the college £100 for the "yea[rly] maintenance of some poor scholler" (Godzicki, 1975, p. 15). This single scholarship embodied many of the characteristics (for example, philanthropic support, aid to the needy) of and set the pattern for student aid programs of the future. Similarly, what was eventually to become the admissions function on college campuses can trace its roots to the Statutes of Harvard College (circa 1646). The first law of Harvard College dealt explicitly with admissions: "When any Scholar is

NEW DIRECTIONS FOR STUDENT SERVICES, no. 89, Spring 2000 © Jossey-Bass Publishers able to Read Tully or such like classical Latin Author *ex tempore,* and make and speak true Latin in verse and prose *suo (ut aiunt) Marte,* and decline perfectly the paradigms of Nouns and verbs in the Greek tongue, then may he be admitted into the College, nor shall any claim admission before such qualifications" ("Statutes," 1989, p. 89).

Early American college enrollment levels were driven not so much by recruiting as by institutional expansion (Coomes, 1994). Prior to the Revolutionary War, higher education consisted of twelve small provincial colleges (for example, in 1770 Harvard only enrolled 413 students) (Brubacher and Rudy, 1997). As the nation expanded westward, colleges would soon follow. This expansion would be facilitated by legislation such as the Survey Ordinance of 1785, which required newly formed townships to set aside plots of land for the development of schools, and the Northwest Ordinance of 1787, which endowed the creation of seminaries of learning. The federal government would also support institution building through the development of the U.S. Military Academy at West Point in 1802 and the Naval Academy at Annapolis in 1845 (Gladieux and Wolanin, 1976).

New institution building was given its greatest impetus with the passage of the two Morrill Acts in 1862 and 1890. Patterned after earlier legislation, these Acts authorized "grants of federal land to each state for the establishment of colleges specializing in agricultural and mechanical arts" ("Federal Education Programs," 1965, p. 1196). In addition to fostering institutional growth, the two Morrill Acts represented a new focus on educational access. A college education was no longer just for the sons of the wealthy, but was intended for the sons of farmers as well. The 1890 Act further extended equity, at least in the letter of the law, by requiring that annual federal grants supporting land grant colleges be withheld from states that did not provide educational opportunities for the newly freed slaves of the southern and boarder states. Most of those states used the law's "separate but equal" provision to create new colleges for African Americans rather than admit them to the existing land grant colleges. This resulted in a two-tiered system of state-supported education in the south, one that was always separate but seldom equal.

Although one can seriously question the success of the Morrill Acts in fostering racial equality, there is no doubt that the Acts ushered in a college-building boom unlike any that had proceeded it. In 1866, there were 467 colleges in the United States (Harris, 1972). By 1870, there were 563 colleges, and by 1880, the number had swelled to 811 (Snyder, Hoffman, and Geddes, 1996).

This expansion of higher education required the development of new administrative functions. Hossler (1996) has traced the evolution of the role of the admissions officer from the campus administrator called the *major beadle* in the medieval university to the office of the campus registrar. In many early American colleges, the recruiting function was assumed by the president and members of the faculty. The president was just as likely to spend time beating the bushes for new students as he was teaching the cap-stone moral philosophy course, or administering the college (Rudolph, 1990).

The Twentieth Century: From Humble Beginnings to Vibrant System

The first ten years of the new century saw a reversal in the institutional growth patterns that had followed the end of the Civil War. The century's first decade saw the number of institutions decline by nearly 3 percent (from 977 to 951). However, the colleges that remained increased in size, as evidenced by a climb in enrollment to 355,213 students in 1910, an increase of 50 percent from 1900 (Snyder, Hoffman, and Geddes, 1996). Enrollments, and the number of institutions, would see steady growth until the onset of the Depression.

Helping facilitate this growth would be a new campus administrator, the dean of admissions. According to Hossler (1996), "The first Deans of Admissions were hired in the 1920s, but the practice did not become widespread until the 1930s" (p. 60). These new deans had the responsibility of assuring that applicants were prepared for college. They began to use objective measures to examine the quality of applicants for admission (Hossler, 1996).

Prior to the 1930s, most scholarships and other tuition benefits were administered by a clerk in the college's business office or by the college bursar. However, in 1933, Smith College created a separate financial aid office (Duffy and Goldberg, 1998). The creation of the Smith College financial aid office marked the beginning of the process of recognizing student aid as an institutional function. While Smith was creating an administrative office focused on student aid, the federal government was implementing a new program of assistance to students. The National Youth Administration (NYA), one of numerous New Deal social programs, was created in 1935. The NYA assisted 620,000 students with $93 million in its eight-year existence (Brubacher and Rudy, 1997). Although it was most accurately called a public works program, the NYA nevertheless helped numerous students earn funds for college. The NYA also represented a slight shift in federal education initiatives. Unlike the Morrill Act that preceded it, the NYA targeted federal assistance not to institutions, but to individual young people. Finally, in its use of federal funds to secure a number of related policy goals, the NYA served as a precursor to the next piece of federal legislation aimed at colleges (Coomes, 1994).

Federal Initiatives and Postwar Boom. College enrollments and institutional growth were to be slowed with the entrance of the United States into World War II. But that event would lead to passage of the Serviceman's Readjustment Act (GI Bill of Rights) in 1944. Like the NYA that preceded it, the GI Bill was intended to accomplish numerous public policy goals, including rewarding veterans for their service and easing the burden on a fragile postwar economy that a significant number of employable men and women represented (Coomes, 1994). The GI Bill was to have a profound impact on higher education. Total college enrollment in 1950 exceeded enrollment levels in 1940 by 1.1 million students, or 78 percent. That influx of new students would require colleges to institute new services and build new facilities, and it would lead to a significant expansion in the number of institutions nationwide.

In 1946, President Truman appointed a commission to examine "the functions of higher education in our democracy and the means by which they can best be performed" (President's Commission on Higher Education, 1947, p. iii). The Commission recommended the removal of all barriers to educational opportunity by doubling college enrollments within a decade. To accomplish that goal, the Commission proposed the establishment in each state of publicly supported "community colleges" to offer free public education through the fourteenth grade. Furthermore, the Commission proposed the development of a national scholarship program that would be made available to nonveteran students (Brubacher and Rudy, 1997).

The policy recommendations formulated by the Truman Commission would be enacted at the federal level by a string of important pieces, beginning with the National Defense Education Act (NDEA). Spurred on by a heightened sense of Cold War competition with the Soviet Union and fears that higher education was failing to meet adequately the manpower needs of an increasingly complex economy, Congress passed the NDEA in 1958. The NDEA contained numerous important education initiatives, not the least of which was the creation of the National Defense Student Loan (NDSL, currently the Federal Perkins Loan). The NDSL program is notable as the first program of generally available student aid. NDEA has been cited as major education legislation for a number of reasons: its emphasis on enhancing quality; its "suggestion that the federal government was moving in the direction of guaranteed opportunity for higher education" (Conlan, 1981, p. 11); and its emphasis on targeting student aid resources to students and not institutions (Coomes, 1994).

Two additional events in the 1950s spurred on the growth of the student aid enterprise. The first was the development of an objective system for assessing the family's ability to pay for a college education—a system that became known as *needs analysis*. The needs analysis process that would be adopted by most colleges in the 1960s was an outgrowth of a system developed by John Monro of Harvard University and the College Scholarship Service (CSS) of the College Board. The College Scholarship Service had been created in 1954 in an attempt to provide more detailed and accurate information to college scholarship committees and to help alleviate bidding wars for highly qualified college applicants (Duffy and Goldberg, 1998). The second event was the development of the financial aid office. The passage of NDEA and the development of a formal needs analysis process fostered the creation of numerous independent offices with the responsibility for establishing eligibility standards, awarding funds, and monitoring the student aid process (Lange, 1983).

The advent of President Johnson's Great Society program was to lead to the most significant period for educational legislation in the twentieth century. The first major student aid program enacted during the Johnson years was the College Work Study program, created as part of the Educational Opportunity Act of 1964. With its emphasis on aiding needy college students through the provision of campus employment opportunities, the College Work Study Program nicely combined the welfare and education goals of the Johnson Great Society.

In 1965, Congress passed the most comprehensive higher education legislation to that time, the Higher Education Act (HEA). The HEA of 1965 authorized the Educational Opportunity Grant program, created a program of guaranteed subsidized student loans (which evolved into today's Federal Family Education Loan program, or FFELP), transferred the College Work Study program from the Office of Educational Opportunity to the Office of Education, and modified the NDSL program.

This landmark legislation, which has become the authorizing legislation for all the federal student aid programs, was passed in a year of unprecedented social legislation. In addition to the HEA, Congress also enacted Medicare, the Voting Rights Act, and the Elementary and Secondary School Act (Gladieux and Wolanin, 1976). By creating the national scholarship program called for by the Truman Commission, the HEA resulted in a comprehensive set of aid programs—grants, loans, and work—to meet the needs of the nation's students. The Higher Education Act firmly committed the federal government to student aid as a vehicle for assuring access to higher education.

Student aid as an institutional function and as a profession would come of age in 1966 with the creation of the National Student Aid Council (Brooks, 1986). The National Student Aid Council, which would become the National Association of Student Financial Aid Administrators (NASFAA), had its roots in the College Board, the College Scholarship Service, Commission V of the American College Personnel Association, and a number of regional student affairs associations (Coomes, 1996). With its emphases on advocacy and professional development, NASFAA would grow into one of the most respected, and largest, higher education associations in Washington, D.C.

By the end of the 1960s, student financial aid was becoming a mature industry. Independent student aid offices existed on many campuses. The passage of the Higher Education Act resulted in a system of federally funded grant, loan, and work programs intended to meet the needs of students. Finally, a national professional association was created to support and train student aid administrators.

The 1970s: Enrollment Management's Nascency. Pushed by significant changes in the demographic makeup of the student body (increasing numbers of women and people of color were attending college), and supported by the post–World War II baby boom, college enrollments had exploded in the 1960s. By 1970, college enrollments had swelled to over 8 million students, an increase of 120 percent over the number enrolled in 1960. To meet the growing demand, more than five hundred new colleges were opened during the 1960s (Snyder, Hoffman, and Geddes, 1996). The continued growth of higher education, however, was to slow during the mid-1970s as the number of high school graduates declined sharply. That decline, and its anticipated negative effects on college enrollments coupled with an emerging body of research on the impact on college on students, was to have a significant effect on the development of enrollment management as a concept and organizational function.

Expanded Goals for Student Aid. In the 1960s, the established goal of the federal student aid programs (and many state aid programs) was the assurance of educational opportunity. Federal financial aid was seen as a vehicle for removing cost as a barrier to higher education attendance. In the 1970s, the goal of access would be broadened to include not just low-income students but middle-income students as well, and would be joined by the goal of assuring students a choice of institution to attend.

To help realize the twin goals of access and choice, Congress enacted the Education Amendments of 1972. From the student aid perspective, the 1972 Education Amendments are important for two reasons: First, they created the Basic Educational Opportunity Grant (BEOG, since renamed the Federal Pell Grant program). The BEOG program was intended to be a portable grant program; grants were made directly to students who could then use them at whatever college they chose to attend. Furthermore, the program was envisioned as an entitlement; BEOG was intended to be the foundation for a student's entire financial aid package, and all eligible students were guaranteed funding within the limits of available appropriations. By committing to the entitlement and portable functions of the Basic Educational Opportunity Grant, the federal government had assured students some level of institutional choice and had given them some control over the admissions process. Second, the Amendments expanded eligibility for participation in the subsidized Guaranteed Student Loan (GSL) program. Low-income students would be assisted through the newly created BEOG program; middle-income students would be aided through participation in the GSL program.

According to Duffy and Goldberg (1998), "The phrase 'middle income squeeze' dominated not only the financial aid reports . . . in the early and mid-1970s but also the national press" (p. 183). Middle-class voters were concerned that tuition rates were rising faster than they could afford and also that they were being locked out of student aid programs targeted at the poor. These concerns caused policymakers to expand the federal student aid programs to meet the needs of a new clientele. Congress had initially responded to the needs of the middle class by liberalizing the needs-analysis formulas as early as 1969 (Duffy and Goldberg, 1998). They had addressed the needs of this vocal constituent group in the Education Amendments of 1972 by expanding eligibility for the GSL program. In 1978, they would further assist middle-class students through passage of the Middle Income Student Assistance Act (MISAA). Prior to passage of MISAA, the benefits of the student aid programs were primarily targeted at students from families with incomes of $15,000 or less. After passage of MISAA, families with adjusted gross incomes of $25,000 or less became eligible to participate in many of the federal (and some state) aid programs. What was most important, however, was that passage of MISAA added a new, and vocal, group of supporters—middle-income families—to the financial aid programs. These families, and their children, would see student aid as an entitlement, a set of programs in which they had a right to participate. No longer was aid simply intended to meet equal opportunity goals, now it was intended to meet the goals of access and institutional choice for students from a wide range of income levels.

Student Persistence as a Field of Study. While federal and state policymakers were developing new initiatives to expand enrollment at the nation's colleges, a new line of research that was targeted at better understanding the impact of the college experience on students was being developed. A number of research studies were conducted in the 1950s and 1960s that attempted to explain why students failed to persist in college. Perhaps the most widely disseminated work on the topic was Summerskill's chapter, "Dropouts from College," in Nevitt Sanford's classic work *The American College: The Psychological and Social Interpretation of the Higher Learning* (1962). Summerskill summarized the findings on the extant research on student attrition and suggested that additional research on student motivation was needed. What was more important, Sanford's book called attention to the role college played in shaping the learning and development of young people and started a process of understanding the impact of college in a more empirical and reasoned manner.

In the 1970s, descriptive studies (for example, Astin, 1972) of college impact and college dropout were augmented by the development of theoretical models explaining the persistence process. In 1975, both Alexander Astin and Vincent Tinto promulgated models to explain why students withdraw from college. Astin (1975), in his research, specifically examined the relationship of the receipt of grants and loans to student persistence and the impact of working on dropping out. In his theory, Tinto (1975) suggested that students enter college with a number of pre-entry attributes (for example, family background and skills and abilities), as well as intentions to complete a college education and a set of institutional and goal commitments. Those intentions are influenced by formal and informal experiences in the institution's academic and social environment. Those experiences determine the student's level of academic and social integration at the institution, which in turn influences the student's decision to stay or depart. The theoretical models developed by Astin and Tinto were to play an important role in generating additional research and new theoretical models, and would influence the development of interventions aimed at keeping students enrolled.

Closely related to the question of why students drop out of college is the question of why students choose to attend college and the factors that influence institutional choice. Like Summerskill (1962), Douvan and Kaye (1962) prepared a chapter, "Motivational Factors in College Entrance," for *The American College.* In the 1970s, research by Corrallo and Davis (1977) and Corwin and Kent (1978), to name just two examples, focused specifically on the role student aid played in the college choice process. Other studies, for example, Craft and Howard (1979), examined the use of student aid as a recruiting tool.

Organizational Responses to Shifting Enrollments. By the mid-1970s, two of the forces that would shape the development of enrollment management as a concept and organizational structure were in place—a complex set of federal, state, and institutional aid programs to support access and choice, and a growing body of empirical research on the college choice process and the factors that influenced student attrition. These two forces would be joined by a third, projections of a significant decline in college enrollments in the mid-1970s, to foster the development of enrollment management as an organizational function.

The early to mid-1970s were a period of considerable unease in campus admissions offices. Projections of enrollment shortages, driven by declining numbers of high school graduates, were cause for concern. Although enrollments did not decline, they failed to grow at the same rates as they had from the end of World War II through the 1960s (Duffy and Goldberg, 1998). Total college enrollment in 1970 was 120 percent higher than enrollment levels in 1960, but from 1970 to 1980 enrollment only increased by 45 percent. Nevertheless, concern over declining high school graduation rates prompted many colleges to look carefully at the role of the admissions office and to consider how better to attract and keep students. One approach was the development of enrollment management as a organizational function.

Hossler (1996) credits Jack McGuire with coining the term *enrollment management* to explain administrative functions that were being put in place at Boston College in the late 1970s to support institutional enrollment goals. Other colleges, including Bradley University, California State University at Long Beach, Carnegie-Mellon University, and Northwestern University, "are generally credited as being among the first institutions to develop comprehensive enrollment management systems" (Hossler, 1996, p. 66).

The 1980s: Enrollment Management Defined and Refined. The concept of enrollment management that had emerged by the late 1970s would be refined and expanded in the early 1980s. In addition, the decade would also see changes in student aid and an expansion of research on the college choice process and student attrition that would have an impact on policy and practice in the 1990s.

Defining Enrollment Management and Studying the Enrollment Process. Early attempts to define formally the term *enrollment management* were undertaken by Kreutner and Godfrey in 1981 and Kemerer, Baldridge, and Green in 1982. In a 1984 book, Hossler suggested that enrollment management incorporates the following activities: (1) student marketing and recruitment; (2) pricing and financial aid; (3) academic and career counseling; (4) academic assistance programs; (5) institutional research; (6) orientation; (7) retention programs; and (8) student services. For additional insight on early enrollment efforts and for a more detailed definition of enrollment management, see Chapter Six.

Enrollment management as an organizational function would continue to be supported by a growing body of research on college choice, student persistence, and the impact of student aid on the two processes. In the 1980s, the theoretical foundations established by Astin and Tinto would be expanded by Bean (1980), Pascarella and Terenzini (1980), Terenzini and Pascarella (1980), Bean and Metzner (1985), and Tinto (1987). The work of Bean and Metzner warrants further discussion because it applied Tinto's theory to the understanding of departure decisions of nontraditional students. During the 1970s and 1980s, nontraditional students and women were primarily responsible for offsetting the anticipated enrollment shortages that were to be brought about by declining high school graduation levels. By focusing their research on nontraditional students, Bean and Metzner were offering insights to researchers and policymakers that recognized the changing shape of the enrollment landscape.

Student Aid in an Era of Retrenchment. The Higher Education Act of 1965 was reauthorized by Congress in 1980. That year would be more famous, however, for the election of Ronald Reagan. With the assumption of the conservative Reagan administration to office, the growth of the student aid programs slowed considerably and a new trend toward increased self-reliance was established. For nearly every year it was in office, the Reagan administration proposed budgets that were lower than the previous year's appropriation levels. However, Congress rejected massive budget cuts for student aid for every fiscal year with the exception of 1981 and 1982 (Eaton, 1991). Nevertheless, the administration's emphasis on reducing the size of the federal budget led to limited growth in student aid funding, resulting in federal student aid appropriations that failed to keep pace with rising college costs or the national rate of inflation (Eaton, 1991).

An important change that would subtly shift the direction of efforts in federal student aid occurred in 1986 with the creation of the congressional methodology for establishing need for federal student assistance (Duffy and Goldberg, 1998). Prior to 1986, the needs analysis formula had been established by the student aid community in conjunction with private organizations such as the College Scholarship Service. After 1986, Congress would set the formula for establishing financial need (and in 1992 extend the congressional methodology to the Pell Grant program). The new congressional methodology, particularly in its treatment of independent students, was more liberal, resulting in a reduction in expected financial contributions. Many colleges felt the need to use formulae other than the more liberal congressional methodology for establishing eligibility for institutional need. This two-tiered needs analysis process resulted in a change in how student eligibility for aid was determined: "When the goals of financial aid were access and choice, financial aid directors wanted award packages received by students from different colleges to be the same so that a student could choose the best place for her on educational grounds alone, regardless of cost. In many ways, . . . there has been a return to the days prior to CSS when there was no uniform method of determining need and aid packages were used as bidding chips for desired students" (Duffy and Goldberg, 1998, p. 201).

Student Aid in the 1990s: From Student Needs to Institutional Desires

The decade of the 1990s can be characterized as one that has emphasized student consumerism, public skepticism about the value of higher education, institutional concerns for fiscal and enrollment viability, and calls for reform of undergraduate education. All these factors would influence student aid policy and ultimately enrollment management decisions.

Student aid legislation in the 1990s would focus on two areas—student loans and tuition-tax credits. The 1990s were truly the decade of student loans. When the Pell Grant was created in 1972, grant assistance was perceived to be the foundation of a student's financial aid award. However, the Reagan administration's concerted efforts to reduce the size of the federal government, an animus toward welfare "grants," and the expansion of the Federal Family Educational Loan Program to include loans for parents and students resulted in stagnant funding for grants and sharp increases in loan funding. In 1998, the College Board noted that "loans now comprise 60 percent of all student aid compared to just over 45 percent ten years ago" (p. 4). Expanded federal loan capacity was greatly facilitated by the creation of the William D. Ford Federal Direct Loan program. Created as a demonstration project by the Higher Education Amendments of 1992, the program was seen as a simpler alternative to the FFELP (originally the Guaranteed Student Loan program). Students could apply for a loan directly from a participating college. In 1994–1995, a total of 104 colleges participated in the program; by the 1997–1998 academic year, that number had increased to 1,350 (U.S. Department of Education, 1998).

The other major federal initiatives of the 1990s were the creation of the Hope Scholarship and Lifetime Learning Credits. These programs were authorized as part of the Balanced Budget Act of 1997 and the Taxpayer Relief Act of 1997. The two programs attempt to expand educational opportunity by providing taxpayers with a tax credit for college expenses. Other tax incentives (for example, a nontaxable educational savings account) were also included in the bills (Kane, 1999). Hope Scholarship and Lifetime Learning Credits are noteworthy for two reasons: (1) They represent a move away from the traditional student aid delivery methods. Through the use of tax credits and other forms of tax relief for educational expenses, the federal government is interacting directly with students and families and not student aid administrators and other members of the student aid industry. (2) They change the target of student assistance. Although tax relief is indexed to income, there is no doubt that the primary targets of the programs are members of the middle class. By targeting the middle-class, the programs continue a process begun with passage of MISAA in 1978, and indicate that "the federal commitment to 'access' for low-income students can no longer be taken for granted" (Spencer, 1999, p. 116).

More so than any substantive policy changes, however, the enrollment and student aid puzzle in the 1990s has been about perceptions. Students, families, and public policymakers perceive college costs to be growing at uncontrollable rates. College and university policymakers perceive increasing competition for students. Educational consumers perceive student aid as an entitlement and a bargaining chip to be used to secure the best possible enrollment conditions. All of these perceptions are grounded in reality.

College costs have risen significantly during the 1990s (see Chapter Three for a discussion of cost increases). But as the National Commission on the Cost of Higher Education (1998) concluded, perceptions of rising college costs should not deter prospective students from seeking a higher education. With the availability of student aid, a college education is well within reach for most Americans.

Competition is fierce for students. Enrollment levels grew at modest rates during the early and mid-1990s. To meet the demand for students, colleges employed sophisticated marketing techniques and econometric models to target aid at groups of students they felt were most likely to meet enrollment goals. Whether they will need to do so in the future remains to be seen. Colleges are just beginning to see the effects of the baby boom "echo" as the children of parents born in the 1950s and 1960s are just beginning to enter college. It is anticipated that by 2004, the number of traditional-aged college students (age eighteen to twenty-four) will increase by 15 percent, or 1.2 million students over the number enrolled in 1993. How individual colleges interpret their own missions and how they see the students in that 15 percent contributing to that mission will determine the enrollment management strategies those colleges employ.

Finally, college applicants have become more savvy. They rely on consultants to assist them in completing student aid and scholarship applications and in structuring their assets to have the least impact on their eligibility for student aid. With the advent of scholarship search engines and other forms of information on the World Wide Web, college applicants have ready access to more information than any previous generation. And as McPherson and Schapiro (1998) note, the rules of the student aid game have changed. When student aid resources were adequate to meet the full need of students and when student aid packages reasonably balanced grants, loans, and student employment, colleges saw aid as a way of assuring access and choice and students saw little need to "negotiate" packages that differed little from institution to institution. However, now that institutions can no longer meet full need and are using their own resources to target the most admissible or most desirable students, applicants recognize that they have the opportunity, and perhaps the right, to bargain for the most favorable student aid award.

Conclusion

The goals and scope of the student aid programs and their relationship to the enrollment process have changed since Lady Ann Radcliff Mowlson endowed the first scholarship at Harvard. The legacy of that first scholarship is a complex array of student aid programs intended to meet a wide array of personal, institutional, and public policy goals. There is no reason to believe that the purposes of student aid will not continue to evolve. What is important, however, is that colleges and public policymakers not shy away from the original goals of the programs—helping the underprivileged secure an education. The positive benefits of a college education are well documented and the nation's human capital needs are too important to warrant departing from those goals.

References

Astin, A. W. *College Dropouts: A National Study.* Washington, D.C.: American Council on Education, 1972.

Astin, A. W. *Preventing Students from Dropping Out.* San Francisco: Jossey-Bass, 1975.

Bean, J. "Dropouts and Turnover: The Synthesis and Test of a Causal Model of Student Attrition." *Research in Higher Education,* 1980, *12,* 155–187.

Bean, J., and Metzner, B. "A Conceptual Model of Nontraditional Undergraduate Student Attrition." *Review of Educational Research,* 1985, *55,* 485–540.

Brooks, S. *NASFAA—The First Twenty Years: An Organizational History of the National Association of Student Financial Aid Administrators.* Washington, D.C.: National Association of Student Financial Aid Administrators, 1986.

Brubacher, J. S., and Rudy, W. *Higher Education in Transition: A History of American Colleges and Universities.* (4th ed.) New Brunswick, N.J.: Transaction, 1997.

Corrallo, S. B., and Davis, J. A. *Impact of Financial Aid on Postsecondary Entrance and Persistence.* Durham: North Carolina Research Triangle Institute, 1977.

College Board. *Trends in Student Aid, 1998.* Washington, D.C.: College Board, 1998.

Conlan, T. J. *The Federal Role in the Federal System: The Dynamics of Growth.* Vol. 6: *The Evolution of a Problematic Partnership: The Feds and Higher Education.* Washington, D.C.: Advisory Commission on Intergovernmental Relations, 1981.

Coomes, M. D. "A History of Federal Involvement in the Lives of Students." In M. D. Coomes and D. D. Gehring (eds.), *Student Services in a Changing Federal Climate.* New Directions for Student Services, no. 68. San Francisco: Jossey-Bass, 1994.

Coomes, M. D. "Student Financial Aid." In A. Rentz (ed.), *Student Affairs Practice in Higher Education.* Springfield, Ill.: Thomas, 1996.

Corwin, T. M., and Kent, L. (eds.). *Tuition and Student Aid: Their Relation to College Entrance Decisions.* Washington, D.C.: American Council on Education, 1978.

Craft, L. N., and Howard, M. D. "Financial Aid: Just a Recruiting Tool?" *Journal of Student Financial Aid,* 1979, *9* (1), 33–38.

Douvan, E., and Kaye, C. "Motivational Factors in College Entrance" In N. Sanford (ed.), *The American College: The Psychological and Social Interpretation of the Higher Learning.* New York: Wiley, 1962.

Duffy, E. A., and Goldberg, I. *Crafting a Class: College Admissions and Financial Aid, 1955–1994.* Princeton, N.J.: Princeton University Press, 1998.

Eaton, J. S. *The Unfinished Agenda: Higher Education in the 1980s.* Old Tappan, N.J.: Macmillan, 1991.

"Federal Education Programs: Federal Aid to Education." In *Congress and the Nation: A Review of Government and Politics in the Post-War Years,* Vol. 1: *1945–1964.* Washington, D.C.: Congressional Quarterly, 1965.

Gladieux, L. E., and Wolanin, T. R. *Congress and the Colleges.* San Francisco: New Lexington Press, 1976.

Godzicki, R. J. "A History of Financial Aids in the United States." In R. Keene, F. C. Adams, and J. E. King (eds.), *Money, Marbles, or Chalk: Student Financial Support in Higher Education.* Carbondale: Southern Illinois University Press, 1975.

Harris, S. E. *A Statistical Portrait of Higher Education.* New York: McGraw-Hill, 1972.

Hossler, D. *Enrollment Management: An Integrated Approach.* New York: College Board, 1984.

Hossler, D. "From Admission to Enrollment Management." In A. Rentz (ed.), *Student Affairs Practice in Higher Education.* Springfield, Ill.: Thomas, 1996.

Kane, T. J. "Student Aid After Tax Reform." In J. E. King (ed.), *Financing a College Education: How It Works, How It's Changing.* Phoenix: Oryx Press, 1999.

Kemerer, F. R., Baldridge, J. V., and Green, K. C. *Strategies for Effective Enrollment Management.* Washington, D.C.: American Association of State Colleges and Universities, 1982.

Kreutner, L., and Godfrey, E. S. "Enrollment Management: A New Vehicle for Institutional Renewal." *College Board Review,* Fall-Winter 1981, pp. 6–9, 29.

Lange, M. L. "Factors in Organizing and Effective Student Aid Office." In R. H. Fenske, R. P. Huff, and Associates, *Handbook of Student Financial Aid.* San Francisco: Jossey-Bass, 1983.

McPherson, M. S., and Schapiro, M. O. *The Student Aid Game: Meeting Need and Rewarding Talent in American Higher Education.* Princeton, N.J.: Princeton University Press, 1998.

National Commission on the Cost of Higher Education. *Straight Talk About College Costs and Prices.* Phoenix: Oryx Press, 1998.

Pascarella, E. T., and Terenzini, P. T. "Predicting Freshman Persistence and Voluntary Dropout Decisions from a Theoretical Model." *Journal of Higher Education,* 1980, *51,* 60–75.

President's Commission on Higher Education. *Higher Education for American Democracy,* Vol. 1: *Establishing the Goals.* Washington, D.C.: U.S. Government Printing Office, 1947.

Rudolph, F. *The American College and University: A History.* Athens: University of Georgia Press, 1990.

Sanford, N. (ed.). *The American College: A Psychological and Social Interpretation of the Higher Learning.* New York: Wiley, 1962.

Snyder, T. D., Hoffman, C. M., and Geddes, C. M. *Digest of Education Statistics, 1996.* Washington, D.C.: National Center for Education Statistics, 1996.

Spencer, A. C. "The New Politics of Higher Education." In J. E. King (ed.), *Financing a College Education: How It Works, How It's Changing.* Phoenix: Oryx Press, 1999.

"Statutes of Harvard." In L. F. Goodchild and H. S. Wechsler (eds.), *ASHE Reader on the History of Higher Education.* Needham Heights, Mass.: Ginn, 1989.

Summerskill, J. "Dropouts from College." In N. Sanford (ed.), *The American College: The Psychological and Social Interpretation of the Higher Learning.* New York: Wiley, 1962.

Terenzini, P., and Pascarella, E. "Toward the Validation of Tinto's Model of College Student Attrition: A Review of Recent Studies." *Research in Higher Education,* 1980, *12,* 271–282.

Tinto, V. "Dropout from Higher Education: A Theoretical Synthesis of Recent Research." *Review of Educational Research,* 1975, *45,* 89–125.

Tinto, V. *Leaving College: Rethinking the Causes and Cures of Student Attrition.* Chicago: University of Chicago Press, 1987.

U.S. Department of Education. *Direct Loans: A History of Direct Loans.* [http://www.ed.gov/offices/OPE/DirectLoan/history.html]. 1998.

MICHAEL D. COOMES is associate professor of higher education and student affairs and chair of the college student personnel program at Bowling Green State University.

2

The demographic, social, and economic forces of the 1990s dramatically altered the higher education operating environment. This chapter provides a policy context within which to consider the emergence of enrollment management in higher education in response to these forces, and calls for a research- and policy-based approach to enrollment management in the future.

Federal and State Aid in the 1990s: A Policy Context for Enrollment Management

Shirley A. Ort

Demographic, social, and economic forces of the last decade dramatically altered the higher education operating environment. Generally, these forces converge at the state level, for the state is the policy venue where most higher education planning occurs. In many states, even private institutions operate within general state guidelines and parameters governing higher education services and delivery.

"The past several years have brought both philosophical and structural changes in federal and state approaches to student financial assistance, which have undoubtedly affected institutional aid programming" (Reindl and Redd, 1999, p. 2). Consequently, the role of student financial aid has changed from supporting traditional goals of "access and choice" to recruiting students and maximizing institutional revenues. This chapter explores these changes, provides a policy context for understanding the emergence of enrollment management policies and practices, and argues that research and policy-driven enrollment management models, not just revenue-driven ones, are necessary to prepare for and address the opportunities and challenges of the future.

The Changing Role of Student Aid: From Isolation to Integration

The role of student aid has changed. Presidents at tuition-dependent private institutions have always kept a close eye on the financial aid office. However, until about a decade ago, the operations of the financial aid office went relatively unnoticed by most public college and university presidents, providing that there were no adverse audit findings. This is no longer the case. A recent survey of 1,200 two-year and four-year public and private institutions, conducted by President Ron Eaglin of Morehead State University, reveals that more than three-quarters of all responding institutions had organized an enrollment management unit on campus (American Association of State Colleges and Universities, 1999). This reorganization has occurred on most campuses in response to what has become an increasingly competitive admissions and financial aid environment. In a report on enrollment management for the College Board, Wikler (1999, p. 4) notes:

> In today's competitive environment, it is a challenge to meet an institution's complex enrollment goals. Price competition makes it hard to predict yield. Different institutions define need differently, making it hard to allocate resources. Competitive pressures are shifting admissions and financial aid calendars forward, placing stress on staff and adding to workload. Merit scholarships eat into scarce financial aid funds, making it hard to help needy students and achieve diversity goals. Discounting for top students forces up prices for others, which makes it harder to attract applicants, intensifies the need to discount, and makes it hard to achieve revenue goals at budgeted cost levels. All these factors force a close working relationship between admissions and financial aid.

Financial aid administrators have become major players in developing and implementing complex institutional marketing, admission, enrollment, and retention strategies. McPherson and Schapiro (1998) summarize this new environment in *The Student Aid Game*: "Universities, beset by their own fiscal problems and by intense competition for highly qualified, fee-paying students, have ceased to think of their financial aid efforts principally as a noble charitable opportunity and have instead come to focus on the financial aid operation as a key strategic weapon both in recruiting students and in maximizing institutional revenues" (p. 1).

Institutional practices changed because the higher education operating environment changed. During the last decade, several factors converged to alter the role of student financial aid in campus planning, recruitment, and retention efforts. The changing role of student aid can best be understood by looking at the collective experience of the states during this decade. State policies largely define the planning environment for higher education. State laws and policies govern public institutions, as well as directly or indirectly influence private institutions. Each state establishes the framework for financing higher education. State legislatures decide the level of appropriations to public higher education institutions (and in some states, assist private institutions) during each budget cycle; and most also support state-funded student aid programs for students attending both public and private institutions, whether for need-based or merit aid (National Association of State Student Grant and Aid Programs, 1998). State support for financing American higher education far surpasses the federal investment. State appropriations to higher education reached $52.8 billion in 1999 (McKeown-Moak, 1999), compared to a federal outlay of $23.2 billion in 1994–1995 (U.S. National Center for Education Statistics, 1997a).

State and federal methods of financing higher education vary significantly. States support institutions primarily, and students secondarily. By appropriating money for its public institutions, states are able to charge students a tuition price that is below real cost. State appropriations for "direct-to-student" forms of student aid, when expressed as a percentage of total higher education appropriations, ranged from a low of .1 percent in Mississippi to a high of 22.8 percent in New York in 1996–1997; the national average was 6.6 percent (National Association of State Student Grant and Aid Programs, 1998). Conversely, the federal government supports students primarily, and institutions secondarily. Federal aid for postsecondary education, with the exception of research grants, is targeted almost exclusively for assistance to financially needy students rather than to institutions. These parallel methods of financing higher education have complemented one another since the inception of federally funded need-based student aid programs in 1965, and have worked well.

Since states provide most of the funding for higher education institutions, they largely define the operating environment. State legislatures and higher education planning authorities establish statewide enrollment goals, determine which populations will have access to postsecondary education (and at which types of institutions), and govern how postsecondary education will be financed. Many states strive for an integrated set of policies necessary to shape the delivery of higher education. These policies establish admissions standards, enrollment goals, tuition rates, diversity goals, student financial aid funding levels, and standards for measuring student achievement and success, and they dictate institutional "performance measures" such as retention and graduation rates. Policy integration at the state level is increasingly important. Similarly, student aid policies are integral to higher education: They influence other policies and are influenced by them.

The past several years have prompted major changes within higher education financing patterns. In the 1990s, policy shifted from public financing of higher education (via appropriations and grants) to student funding (via higher tuition and borrowing) (Reindl and Redd, 1999). Loans now comprise 60 percent of all aid, compared to just 45 percent ten years ago (College Board, 1998b). Additionally, the focus of state student aid continues to move from need-based aid to merit-based aid. Between 1995–1996 and 1996–1997, states increased their spending on need-based aid programs by only 5 percent but boosted their spending on merit programs by 12 percent (National Association of State Student Grant and Aid Programs, 1998). During the 1998 legislative sessions, twelve states adopted some form of a merit-based scholarship program, in many cases modeled on the Georgia Hope Scholarship (McKeown-Moak, 1999). Today all but a few states have merit scholarship programs in place (National Association of State Student Grant and Aid Programs, 1998).

Institutional aid has become an increasingly important source of financial aid for students and their families. Collectively, public and private institutions more than doubled institutional aid from 1988 to 1998 (College Board, 1998b). Institutional aid increased from 14 percent of financial aid awarded from all sources in 1990 to 18 percent by 1996 (Reindl and Redd, 1999). Driven by bidding wars, institutions found it necessary to raise tuition, discount prices in order to leverage additional enrollments, and infuse additional merit money. The desire to improve institutional rankings published annually by *U.S. News and World Report, Kiplinger's,* or *Money* drove much of the increase in aid provided by institutions. Improved rankings would almost certainly increase institutional stature, reputation, and hence desirability. Institutional wealth had little to do with this trend. According to one author, "The granting of institutional aid is no longer a function of institutional wealth but has become an enrollment management tool. The granting of aid to a significant percent of the class is a necessary tool to fill the class with the number and quality of students that are necessary" (Lapovsky, 1999, pp. 299–300).

A retrospective look at some of the causes of these changes may prove useful and provide a framework for a better understanding of how institutional competition became so keen and campus enrollment management units so common.

The State Policy Venue: Changing Conditions

Demographic shifts, social forces, and economic pressures of the 1990s provoked dramatic changes in higher education, ushering in enrollment management practices as we know them today. Financial pressures drove many of these changes. As one state higher education executive officers' report claims, "It was the best of times; it was the worst of times" (McKeown-Moak, 1999, p. 1).

Demographics.   The demographic changes of the early 1990s resulted in fewer students graduating from high school. After reaching an all-time high of 3.1 million high school graduates nationally in 1978–1979, the number dropped steadily for several years and did not start to rise again until 1993–1994 (Western Interstate Commission on Higher Education, 1998). A decreasing number of high school graduates equaled fewer students directly pursuing postsecondary education, making it more difficult for a number of institutions to meet their enrollment goals.

National data obscure regional trends, which reveal that different parts of the country experienced varying birth rates and shifting populations at the outset of the decade. States in the West and Southwest, promising warmer climates and better jobs, attracted residents from the East and the Plains states. The demographics of many states changed, particularly in the West and Southwest, which began to reflect greater racial and ethnic diversity.

In high-growth states, state lawmakers found that more enrollment spaces were needed; capacity was in short supply. Conversely, in states with declining populations, whether due to out-migration or lower birth rates, both public and private institutions scrambled to fill classrooms and avoid the resulting loss of tuition revenue. In an effort to improve market position, institutions raised tuition, offered "discounted" prices to some students while trying to "leverage" the enrollment of other students. These stepped-up efforts meant that competitive financial aid packages became an increasingly important part of an institution's effort to enhance its market position (Dennis, 1998).

Enrollment pressures in many, though not all, states are subsiding today. Higher education institutions across much of the country embrace long-awaited enrollment growth, driven by increases in the number of high school graduates and rising postsecondary education participation rates. In 1993–1994, the number of high school graduates began to rise, and is expected to reach a historical peak of 3.2 million in 2007–2008. This represents a 30 percent increase over the low point in the late 1970s (Western Interstate Commission on Higher Education, 1998). Participation rates are rising as well. In 1977, 50 percent of all high school graduates went on to college; today the rate has climbed to 67 percent (U.S. National Center for Education Statistics, 1997b). Higher education researchers project that enrollment will grow from an estimated 13.9 million in 1995 to 16.1 million by 2007–2008, an increase of 16 percent (U.S. National Center for Education Statistics, 1997b).

According to a *New York Times* article, this projection of increased demand for higher education appears to have commenced already. A number of highly qualified high school seniors applying for fall 1999 admission were rejected by colleges of their choice, leading the author to label this college application season the "most competitive in the nation's history" (Bronner, 1999, p. A1). It is noteworthy, given the backdrop of 1990s, that the term *competitive* describes the process from the standpoint of the student rather than the institution. Bronner (1999) goes on to report that in fall 1999, the number of students enrolled in four-year institutions of higher education was at an all-time high of 14.8 million, up from the record of 14.6 million in fall 1998.

Social Forces. Changing social forces in the 1990s imposed significant budget pressures on states. Population growth and population shifts among states significantly increased demand for public schools and social services such as welfare, health care, and prisons in many states (Western Interstate Commission on Higher Education, 1998). Increased social service caseloads rapidly demanded a larger share of state budgets, depleting budget reserves and "rainy day" funds. The needs of higher education remained pressing, but perhaps less urgent than schooling children, meeting welfare payrolls, or building prisons. Between 1990 and 1994, only seven states increased higher education spending as a proportion of total state spending, whereas thirty-six states increased the share of spending devoted to corrections programs (Ambrosio and Schiraldi, 1997).

Prisons and corrections costs consumed state appropriations at an alarming pace. State prison budgets grew twice as fast as spending on public colleges and universities (Phinney, 1998). For the first time, in 1995, states collectively spent more to construct prisons than they spent on all of higher education, reporting a near dollar-for-dollar tradeoff that year (Ambrosio and Schiraldi, 1997). This increase in the corrections budget was driven by growth in the young adult populations, high unemployment leading to increased criminal activity, and the adoption of more stringent sentencing guidelines (Ambrosio and Schiraldi, 1997).

At the close of the decade, conditions have improved. Crime rates appear to be stabilizing or moving slightly downward (Ambrosia and Schiraldi, 1997). Federal welfare reform legislation, enacted in 1996, resulted in reduced caseloads in nearly every state and created a windfall of federal monies in some states. Since January 1996, welfare rolls have dropped 27 percent nationwide; in eight states, caseloads have declined by more than 40 percent during the past year (National Association of State Budget Officers, 1998). These recent changes have begun to ease some of the stresses placed on state budgets earlier in the decade.

Economics.   States were financially unprepared for the demographic and social changes of the 1990s. Tax resources were slim even before the onslaught of new budget pressures. The economy was lagging: growth in per capita income had slowed or was declining in some regions. Taxpayers balked over the prospect of new taxes; consequently, state revenues failed to keep pace with increased demands for state services. Competing budget pressures caused a reduction in funding for higher education. As a result, state appropriations for public higher education declined by 8 percent in inflation-adjusted dollars between 1989–1990 and 1995–1996 (American Association of State Colleges and Universities, 1998).

In response to diminishing state support, public institutions sought and attained greater authority over their tuition policies, and raised tuition accordingly (Davis, 1997; Mumper, 1997; U.S. General Accounting Office, 1998; McPherson and Schapiro, 1998; and Education Resources Institute, 1998). A recent U.S. General Accounting Office study (1998) reported that for every dollar lost in state tax revenues, public institutions have raised tuition 75 cents. Over the ten-year period ending in 1998–1999, after adjusting for inflation, average public four-year tuition and fees rose 53 percent compared to 35 percent for private four-year colleges and universities (College Board, 1998a).

At the close of the decade, states are in a much-improved position. Spending, in most states, remains within budget projections, and nearly all states anticipate surpluses by the close of 1999 budget cycles. Combined with similar good news for local governments, state and local governments now take in about $100 billion a year more than they spend (*State Budget and Tax News,* 1999).

A healthy national economy continues to mean good news for state and federal finances. According to the U.S. Congressional Budget Office (1999), "Total federal revenues exceeded spending in fiscal year 1998 by $70 billion, producing the first surplus in almost 30 years" (p. xiii). This improved condition affords state legislatures and Congress the enviable choice among tax cuts, health reserves, debt reduction, or spending increases.

The improvement in state finances has benefited higher education institutions. According to data collected in the annual survey of State Higher Education Finance Officers, state appropriations for higher education reached their highest levels ever in fiscal year 1999: Total state appropriations for FY 1999 reached $52.8 billion, an increase of $3.2 billion, or 6.5 percent, over FY 1998, and a $6.2 billion, or 13.3 percent, increase over FY 1997 (McKeown-Moak, 1999). Currently, states are in the best fiscal health of the decade.

Despite the improvement in state and federal finances, parents, students, and the general public continue to protest the dramatic tuition increases of the decade, enacted in "the worst of times," with cries that higher education is no longer affordable. These cries are the harbinger of increased legislative and congressional oversight of American higher education.

Toward a New Decade: Accountability and Productivity

Spiraling public tuition rates in the 1990s (prompted by reduced state appropriations for higher education), coupled with a prior decade of increases among private colleges and universities, angered students and families and dominated the press. By 1997, legislative concerns and public sentiment coalesced around the issue of rising college costs. This led to the passage of federal legislation creating a National Commission on the Cost of Higher Education (P. L. 105-18). The Commission, first envisioned by Congress in the 1992 Amendments of the Higher Education Act, was given the task of conducting a comprehensive review of college costs and prices. The commission was to examine and make recommendations regarding tuition rates; methods of reducing or stabilizing tuition; trends in college and university administrative costs; trends in faculty workload and remuneration; the condition of higher education facilities; the extent to which increased institutional financial aid and tuition discounting have affected tuition increases; the extent to which government regulations contribute to increased tuition and higher education costs; the establishment of a mechanism for better informing the public about tuition and higher education costs; the extent to which financial aid programs have contributed to changes in tuition; trends in state fiscal policies that have affected college costs; and the adequacy of existing federal and state financial aid programs in meeting the costs of attending colleges and universities (National Commission on the Cost of Higher Education, 1998). The commission published its findings and recommendations in January 1998. Beginning in academic year 2000–2001, the federal government will require institutions to report instructional cost data and student financial aid information. Institutions may be fined up to $25 thousand for failing to report timely and accurate information.

National concern about the escalating cost of higher education continues to command attention by the press. Many believe that institutions can find new efficiencies that will correct or curtail recent growth in tuition rates. However, given the demographic and enrollment projections for the next decade, higher education faces the enormous challenge of delivering increased and improved educational services to larger and more diverse groups of students, without the certainty of significant budget increases or the public's willingness to incur higher tuition charges. Although state appropriations for higher education have increased over the last two years, higher education officials are preparing for reductions in appropriations and increases in the use of performance measures and other "accountability" requirements (McKeown-Moak, 1999).

Accountability and productivity issues continue to dominate discussion of higher education at the state level. New resources, it appears, must be earned. As of 1998, thirty-four states had adopted some form of accountability budgeting or performance funding to ensure that public dollars on education are well spent (McKeown-Moak, 1999). Performance budgeting is a resource allocation method that dispenses state funds based on results, rather than simply renewing prior-year allocations. In states that use performance budgeting, legislative directives typically instruct institutions to assess and report the quality of their education programs as a condition of funding. Legislators want assurance that faculties are teaching (faculty productivity) and students are learning (outcomes assessment). However these new performance measures are established or implemented, the watchword in higher education is *accountability,* the new "scarlet A."

The Campus Planning Environment: Institutional Strategies and Savvy Consumers

Competing claims and interests merge at the campus level where financial aid administrators strive to reconcile institutional enrollment goals, family expectations, available funds, and the dictates of government. These factors align as institutions distribute aid through various student aid packaging policies and constructs.

For many financial aid administrators, the highly competitive and strategic enrollment practices of the past, though deemed necessary, created discomfort. Packaging financial aid has become a major competitive tactic (Wikler, 1999). These changes leave many student aid professionals reaching for "'the ability to deal with disequilibria'—to do something different when the occasion demands," as one author puts it (Schultz, 1975, in McPherson and Schapiro, 1990, p. 20).

Students and families responded to the changes of the last decade as savvy consumers; many learned that some institutions will consider willingness to pay, not just ability to pay, when awarding aid. "To an unprecedented degree they are making their college selection choices based on image and value, as pragmatic consumers" (Spiegler, 1998, p. 52). The process by which students and families choose a college has become much more money-driven than in prior years (Spiegler, 1998). Value, defined as net price in relation to prestige, drives selection of institutions among freshmen and their parents.

However, students may be shortsighted in interpreting value to mean solely price and prestige. The real determination of value is made after a student enrolls at an institution. A broader definition of value might encompass issues such as the ability to participate in campus leadership or honors programs, study abroad or import Internet courses into a customized academic program, gain academically or career related student employment, or access the necessary academic advising and course sequencing to graduate on time. Nevertheless, today's public largely defines value as price relative to institutional selectivity or prestige.

Clearly, colleges and universities do not administer student aid programs in a vacuum. As has been discussed in this chapter, changes in institutional funding and practices are greatly affected by the larger higher education operating environment as well as the choices of federal and state policymakers. Of the latter, "campus leadership must be able to anticipate how current and potential federal and state policy directions may affect their award patterns, as well as how changes in these policies can affect the expectations of potential recipients" (Reindl and Redd, 1999, p. 10).

Looking Ahead: Policy, Practice, and Research

The tuition pricing and aid awarding strategies of the past may prove too limiting to manage the opportunities and the challenges of the future. Numerous pressures and complexities assault the higher education operating environment. Specific developments in the 1990s, including too few high school graduates, too little state and federal money for higher education, and what appeared to be an oversupply of American higher education, fueled the enrollment management practices of that decade. Among other things, the intense competition of the 1990s taught us that in a resource-constrained higher education environment, policy will generally inform practice only where there is an economic benefit to the institution. Most "policy" employed by institutions had a singular goal: Increase net tuition revenue while enhancing the quality measures of the institution.

With the prospect of better times ahead, campuses may now choose to place increased focus on research and apply the results in meaningful ways to campus planning. Jerry Davis (1997) highlights the value of such research in a recent manual for aid administrators, published by the National Association of Student Financial Aid Administrators (NASFAA). Research (1) increases knowledge, responsibility, and control over problems and activities; (2) discloses the effects (both intended and unintended) of financial aid policies and practices; and (3) encourages administrators to question attitudes and beliefs through quantitative analysis.

The relationship of financial aid to student persistence rates provides an example where research can inform policy to the advantage of both students and institutions. Research demonstrates that student aid positively affects persistence and that various types and combinations of aid can enhance that general effect (Tinto, 1975; St. John, 1989, 1991; St. John, Kirshstein, and Noell, 1991; St. John, Andrieu, Oescher, and Starkey, 1994; Somers, 1994). Recent studies have found that adequate aid equalizes the probability of persistence for low-income students and students of color, controlling for other background and educational variables that influence persistence (St. John, 1999; St. John, Hu, Clements, Asker, and Weber, 1999). Furthermore, various aid types have differing effects on low-income students, students of color, students by class level, and students within-year and from year to year (McPherson and Schapiro, 1991; St. John, Andrieu, Oescher, and Starkey, 1994). Individual campuses could test these findings and legislatures could employ the results to form or redirect policies to serve both students and institutions better.

Continuing research on these and related issues can and will inform institutional, state, and federal policies about the value and effects of student aid (and aid distribution patterns) on student access, learning, and achievement. Congressional oversight of college costs and instructional cost containment measures may require as much.

The picture looks brighter for institutions as we enter a new decade. A recent *New York Times* article summarizes current trends: "A roaring economy, a population boom, an increasingly sophisticated education industry, and a growing belief that college is necessary for success have raised the stakes for acceptance to the nation's better colleges. And there is every indication that the trend will intensify over the next ten years" (Bronner, 1999, p. A1).

The article goes on to say that "colleges that a decade ago worried about finding enough good students are now happily overwhelmed" (Bronner, 1999, p. A11).

Summary and Conclusions

The next decade appears to be one of great opportunity. We must reform the practices of the past, inform policies through research, and increasingly apply policy to our decision making. The nation's significantly improved economy creates a new opportunity to fund need-based grants adequately, which can be appropriately complemented by tax credits and merit assistance. However, deliberate action and a broader public policy agenda are needed to protect the statutory purposes of state and federal need-based programs from the skirmishes of the "student aid game," as McPherson and Schapiro call it. Someone needs to worry about "the whole."

Congress and state legislatures have both the privilege and the responsibility for doing so. Reflecting on institutional behaviors of the past and looking toward a brighter future, lawmakers are well positioned to reinterpret and safeguard traditional goals of access and choice. This does not mean that the methods must remain the same, but rather that the goals still need to be fulfilled.

Congress should increase appropriations for need-based grant aid, and reverse two decades of policy drift toward loans. It should do this by increasing grant support to needy students equal to its investment in tax credits for middle-income students and families. Congress took a bold step in 1972 when it first authorized the Pell Grant program and ensured that funding would follow needy students to institutions of their choosing. In so doing, the program supported both access and choice, and created greater equity among students. Congress should hold firm to this program design and resist any effort to block-grant funds to states or institutions, as is currently under consideration for secondary education. Any effort to block-grant funds would most certainly weaken efforts to serve low-income students and students of color. With block grants, institutions, guided by their own enrollment goals or chase for national rankings, could easily subordinate federal need-based aid to self-serving purposes.

Similarly, states with centrally administered grant programs aimed at low-income students should resist campus pressures to decentralize the awarding process. A state has a choice: It can target specific populations and let the dollars follow the students (as with the Federal Pell Grant program) or it can allocate financial aid funds to institutions. However, allocating funds to institutions presents two possible challenges to the goal of equity. First, states may sacrifice equity goals if they disburse grant funds to individual campuses in proportion to institutional enrollments, because a flagship campus almost certainly enrolls a much lower proportion of needy students than a community college. Second, if states allow institutions to determine student eligibility criteria, institutional administrators may subordinate equity concerns to campus enrollment goals aimed at little more than increasing net tuition revenue. To the extent that lawmakers anticipate institutional responses under varying market conditions, they can perhaps mitigate some of the mischief witnessed throughout the last decade.

States also need to reexamine their rush to create new merit scholarship programs. States find it easy to copy the innovation of another, frequently overlooking geographic differences. A Douglas fir may thrive in

Seattle and die in Amarillo. This is not to say that merit-based aid is intrinsically bad, but that states have a threshold obligation to ensure sufficient grant support to protect access.

Institutions, too, should reassess the growing use of their own funds for merit aid programs. A "better input, better output" approach could pose significant challenges to the furtherance of equal educational opportunity. Lower-income students are usually less well prepared academically, scoring lower on standardized tests such as the ACT and SAT, often due to the lack of resources and familial support that facilitates learning (Mortenson, 1998). In the current wake of performance budgeting, merit aid may strike institutions as an ideal way to elevate admissions standards to meet accountability measures with the least investment of new resources. However, institutions must exercise caution to ensure that in the rush to achieve one goal they do not sacrifice another.

State and federal governments should also forge new, mutually reinforcing, partnerships with institutions that serve broader public policy goals. The National Early Intervention and Scholarship Program (NEISP), replaced in the 1998 Higher Education Amendments by the Gaining Early Awareness and Readiness for Undergraduate Programs (GEAR UP), is a prime example of a successful partnership. As a condition of receiving grant funding, states must match the value of the Pell Grant for individual students participating in the program. Through this requirement, Congress assures that low-income and disadvantaged students receive significant grant support, thus increasing the probability of student retention and success. States could apply this model to their own outreach programs by requiring colleges and universities to provide matching grants from institutional sources.

Campus administrators should consciously reflect on the historic purposes and goals of state and federal need-based student aid programs, assessing both moral and monetary implications of institutional policy responses. Institutional financial aid strategies define who we are and, at times, those strategies may not be consistent with the mission of the institution or the public trust placed in institutions by state and federal lawmakers.

The improved demographic, social, and economic conditions at the close of this decade present institutions and lawmakers with an ideal opportunity to reform past practices and strengthen the nation's future equity agenda for higher education. However, deliberate action is needed. Without joined efforts and renewed leadership, society can expect a repeat of the monetary and social costs it incurred in the 1990s. If this reoccurs, the progress of the past would represent little more than a footnote of social conscience in the annals of American higher education.

Four decades have passed since the authorization of the Higher Education Act of 1965, the bedrock of equal opportunity in higher education. The decade ahead unfolds another opportunity to define the American dream, to paint a new landscape over an old canvas of faded promises and blurred vision.

In the words of the late Terry Sanford (1999, p. 14), an alumnus of the University of North Carolina at Chapel Hill, former governor of the state of North Carolina, previous president of Duke University, and U.S. senator (D, N.C.): "It is the genius of America that we can say to all of our young people: If you have the will and the skill, we will not let lack of money deny you a college education. That open door is one of the great promises of the American dream, and it is the foundation of the future strength of the country."

References

Ambrosio, T. J., and Schiraldi, V. *From Classrooms to Cell Blocks: A National Perspective.* Washington, D.C.: Justice Policy Institute, 1997. [http://www.cjcj.org/jpi/highernational.html].

American Association of State Colleges and Universities. *College Costs and Student Financial Aid, 1989–1990 to 1997–1998.* Washington, D.C.: American Association of State Colleges and Universities, 1998.

American Association of State Colleges and Universities. *The Role of College Presidents in Recruitment and Retention.* Washington, D.C.: American Association of State Colleges and Universities, 1999. [http://www.aascu.org/analysis/presidents-recruitment].

Bronner, E. "For '99 College Applicants, Stiffest Competition Ever." *New York Times,* June 12, 1999, pp. A1, A11.

College Board. *Trends in College Pricing.* Washington, D.C.: College Board, 1998a.

College Board. *Trends in Student Aid.* Washington, D.C.: College Board, 1998b.

Davis, J. S. (ed.), *Student Aid Research: A Manual for Financial Aid Administrators.* Washington, D.C.: National Association of Student Financial Aid Administrators, 1997.

Dennis, M. J. *A Practical Guide to Enrollment and Retention Management in Higher Education.* Westport, Conn.: Bergin & Garvey, 1998.

Education Resources Institute and the Institute for Higher Education Policy. *Do Grants Matter? Student Grant Aid and College Affordability.* Boston: Education Resources Institute and the Institute for Higher Education Policy, 1998.

Lapovsky, L. "An Enrollment Management Tool." *NACUBO Business Officer,* 1999, 32 (9), 25–31.

McKeown-Moak, M. P. *Financing Higher Education: An Annual Report from the States.* Denver: State Higher Education Executive Officers, 1999. [http://www.sheeo.org/SHEEO/2306.htm].

McPherson, M. S., and Schapiro, M. O. *Selective Admission and the Public Interest.* Vol. 20. New York: College Entrance Exam Board, 1990.

McPherson, M. S., and Schapiro, M. O. "Does Student Aid Affect College Enrollment? New Evidence on a Persistence Controversy." *America Economic Review,* 1991, 81, 309–318.

McPherson, M. S., and Schapiro, M. O. *The Student Aid Game: Meeting Need and Rewarding Talent in American Higher Education.* Princeton, N.J.: Princeton University Press, 1998.

Mortenson, T. "Chance for College for Students from Low Income Families by State in 1996–1997." *Postsecondary Education Opportunity,* Dec. 1998, pp. 3–7.

Mumper, M. "State Efforts to Keep Public Colleges Affordable in the Face of Fiscal Stress." In J. C. Smart, (ed.), *Higher Education: Handbook of Theory and Research.* Vol. 13. New York: Agathon, 1997.

National Association of State Budget Officers. *Fiscal Survey of the States.* Washington, D.C.: National Association of State Budget Officers, 1998.

National Association of State Student Grant and Aid Programs. *28th Annual Survey Report.* Albany: New York State Higher Education Services Corporation, 1998. [http://www.nassgap.org/research&surveys/28threport.htm].

National Commission on the Cost of Higher Education. *Straight Talk About College Costs and Prices.* Phoenix: Oryx Press, 1998.

Phinney, D. "Prison Funding Explodes in Growth." [http://more.abcnews.go.com/sections/us/DailyNews/prisoneducation980707.html]. 1998.

Reindl, T., and Redd, K. *Institutional Aid in the 1990s: The Consequences of Policy Connections.* Paper presented at the 16th annual Research Network Conference sponsored by the National Association of State Student Grant and Aid Programs and the National Council for Higher Education Loan Programs, Savannah, Ga., May 1999.

St. John, E. P. "The Influence of Student Aid on Persistence." *Journal of Student Financial Aid,* 1989, *19* (3), 52–68.

St. John, E. P. "The Impact of Student Financial Aid: A Review of Recent Research." *Journal of Student Financial Aid,* 1991, *21* (1), 18–32.

St. John, E. P. "Evaluating State Grant Programs: A Case Study of Washington's Grant Program." *Research in Higher Education,* 1999, *40,* 149–170.

St. John, E. P., Andrieu, S. C., Oescher, J., and Starkey, J. B. "The Influence of Student Aid on Within-Year Persistence by Traditional College-Age Students in Four-Year Colleges." *Research in Higher Education,* 1994, *35,* 455–480.

St. John, E. P., Kirshstein, R. J., and Noell, J. "The Effects of Student Financial Aid on Persistence: A Sequential Analysis." *Review of Higher Education,* 1991, *14,* 383–406.

St. John, E. P., Hu, S., Clements, M., Asker, E., and Weber, J. "Keeping Public Colleges Affordable: The Influence of State Grants on Persistence in Indiana Public Higher Education." Presented at the 16th annual Research Network Conference sponsored by the National Association of State Student Grant and Aid Programs and the National Council for Higher Education Loan Programs, Savannah, Ga., May 1999.

Sanford, T. "Special Insights from the Hill: A Bilateral Perspective." *Educational Record,* 1990, *71,* 13–14.

Somers, P. A. "The Effect of Price on Within-Year Persistence." *Journal of Student Financial Aid,* 1994, *24* (1), 31–45.

Spiegler, M. "Have Money, Will Matriculate." *American Demographics,* 1998, *20* (9), 51–56.

State Budget and Tax News, 1999, *18*(5). Birmingham, Ala.: State Policy Research. Inc.

Tinto, V. "Dropout from Higher Education: A Theoretical Synthesis of Recent Research." *Review of Educational Research,* 1975, *45,* 89–125.

U.S. Congressional Budget Office. *The Economic and Budget Outlook, Fiscal Years 2000–2009.* Washington, D.C.: U.S. Congressional Budget Office, 1999.

U.S. General Accounting Office. *Higher Education Tuition Increases and Colleges' Efforts to Contain Costs.* Washington, D.C.: U.S. General Accounting Office, 1998.

U.S. National Center for Education Statistics. "Current Funds Revenues and Expenditures of Institutions of Higher Education: Fiscal Years 1987 to 1995." [http://nces.ed.gov/pubs/cfre97/97441.html]. 1997a.

U.S. National Center for Education Statistics. "Projections of Education Statistics to 2007/Highlights." [http://nces.ed.gov/NCES/pubs/pj/p97001.html]. 1997b.

Western Interstate Commission on Higher Education. "Is Access to College in Jeopardy in the West? Projections of High School Graduates to 2012." [http://www.wiche.edu]. 1998.

Wikler, J. "Enrollment Management: A Report for the College Board—Summary of Findings." Paper presented at a meeting of the College Scholarship Service, New York City, May 1999.

SHIRLEY A. ORT is associate provost and director of scholarships and student aid at the University of North Carolina at Chapel Hill. Previously she served as deputy director for student financial aid at the Washington State Higher Education Coordinating Board.

3

This chapter reviews the issues often involved in shaping institutional financial aid policy and suggests a number of questions for future policy development.

Enrollment Management, Institutional Resources, and the Private College

Joseph A. Russo, Michael D. Coomes

As the nation's colleges enter the twenty-first century, they are faced with a number of critical issues that will shape institutional enrollments and have the potential to affect institutional mission. The role of student aid in the enrollment management equation is critical to ensuring optimal enrollments and a steady revenue stream—a revenue stream campuses must maintain if they wish to meet multiple institutional priorities. In addition, institutions are faced with a number of external demands that complicate institutional responses, including increasing governmental intervention, the rapid diversification of the nation's population, and a student aid system that has become overly complex. Perhaps none of these issues has gained as much attention as the issue of rising college costs. Rising college costs and the concern of many parents about the affordability of higher education for their children have created a significant challenge for the modern American family. Shifts in public subsidies for higher education, a change in the federal student aid system from grants to loans, and an expanding economy also contribute to the demands for more or less student assistance. All these factors shape how institutions will be able to respond to the challenges of maintaining a stable enrollment. Central to that response is the role that institutionally funded sources of assistance play in meeting the needs of students. This chapter focuses on institutional financial aid initiatives that have an impact on the recruitment and retention of students. Topics include the challenges faced by independent colleges, fiscal responses to those challenges, and how colleges can modify their organizational structures to respond to student needs more effectively.

NEW DIRECTIONS FOR STUDENT SERVICES, no. 89, Spring 2000   © Jossey-Bass Publishers

The Unique Challenges Facing Private Higher Education

Private (or independent) colleges and universities exist in the same national context and are confronted with the same dynamics that confront public institutions. Private colleges are subject to the same regulatory demands, they must draw their student bodies from the same pools of high school graduates and adult learners, and they must adhere to the same standards established by regional, national, and professional accrediting agencies. Private colleges must respond to all these conditions while funding their activities without the benefit of public subsidies. The fact that private colleges are tuition-driven has resulted in a process that requires private colleges to increase their tuition levels to meet increased institutional costs. The issues of costs, price, and subsidies have become important and shape numerous institutional policy decisions, including those that attempt to balance quality and equality and assure access and choice. This section examines the issues of cost and price, equality of opportunity, and institutional choice

Cost and Price: Understanding the Terrain.   The past few years have seen increased consternation among a variety of publics with the rapidly rising costs of higher education (Clotfelter, 1996; National Commission on the Cost of Higher Education, 1998; Vogelstein, 1998). Much of that consternation is a result of rapidly escalating cost, but it is exacerbated by lack of understanding by the general public of the difference between cost and price and the role public subsidies play in keeping costs low at public institutions. The National Commission on the Cost of Higher Education notes that defining the terms *cost, price,* and *general subsidy* "is not just a technical sidenote, of interest only to policy analysts" but rather "a major semantic challenge . . . in our national discussion of college costs" (National Commission on the Cost of Higher Education, 1998, p. 3).

The commission developed the following definitions to address the problem (National Commission on the Cost of Higher Education, 1998, p. 4):

Costs: "What institutions spend to provide an education and related educational services to students." This includes *cost per student,* which is the average amount institutions spend annually per each full-time equivalent student.

Price: "What students and families are charged and what they pay." The commission defined *price* in three ways: (1) *Sticker price,* the amount of tuition and fees that colleges charge students to attend and the amount colleges list in their publications; (2) *total price of attendance,* a more encompassing term that includes not just tuition and fees but all the costs a student incurs to attend a particular college, including housing expenses, books, transportation, and miscellaneous expenses; (3) *net price,* the amount "students pay after financial aid has been subtracted from the total price of attendance."

The commission differentiated between two types of net price: "The first measure subtracts *only grants* from the total price of attendance. This concept provides a measure of *affordability*, or the amount of money a student actually pays to attend college. The second measure subtracts *all financial aid awarded*—grants, loans, and work study—from the total price of attendance, to measure the amount of money a student needs in order to enter the college or university. This concept provides a measure of *access*, because, even though loans must be repaid, they allow a student to attend college."

General subsidy: "The difference between the cost to the institution of providing an education ('cost per student') and the tuition charged to students ('sticker price')." Whether students attend public or private institutions or receive any type of student assistance, they benefit from receiving a general subsidy. The amount of that general subsidy differs greatly from college to college with students attending public colleges receiving large state-supported general subsidies.

As the commission noted: "It is important to make a clear distinction between expenditures that *institutions incur* in order to provide an education (costs) and the expenses that *students and families face* (prices)." The failure to understand this distinction has led to considerable confusion on the part of consumers. The need to address this confusion was one of the commission's major recommendations.

Two additional areas of the cost commission's research bear consideration: the evidence of increasing costs in higher education, and conclusions about the factors driving up college costs. Table 3.1 displays average annual tuition and fees for colleges for the period 1988–1989 to 1998–1999 (College Board, 1998). As the table indicates, total dollar increases for tuition and fees (not including room and board charges) were greatest at four-year private colleges ($3,730). Although the *amount* of the increase may influence consumers as they contemplate the sticker price of a college education, it was public colleges that saw the largest *percentage* increase in average tuition and fees during the past decade.

According to data from the 1996 National Postsecondary Student Aid Study, net price calculations showed similar increases for the period 1987 to 1996. Table 3.2 displays net price data for the period 1987 to 1996. As

Table 3.1. Average Annual Tuition and Fees for Undergraduates in Constant Dollars, 1988–1989 to 1998–1999

Sector	1988–1989 ($)	1998–1999 ($)	10-Year Change ($)	10-Year Change %
Two-year public	1,076	1,633	557	52
Four-year public	2,125	3,243	1,118	53
Four-year private	10,778	14,504	3,730	35

Source: Adapted from College Board (1998)

Table 3.2. Changes in Net Prices, 1987–1996

	Public Four-Year			Private Four-Year			Public Two-Year		
	1987 ($)	1996 ($)	Change %	1987 ($)	1996 ($)	Change %	1987 ($)	1996 ($)	Change %
Total price minus grants	4,385	9,365	+114	8,307	15,069	+81	2,345	6,067	+159
Total price minus all aid	3,715	7,262	+95	6,823	11,205	+64	2,125	5,717	+169

Source: Adapted from National Commission on the Cost of Higher Education (1998)

Table 3.2 indicates, although private four-year colleges have the highest sticker prices (in terms of both tuition and fees and total cost of attendance), when net prices are considered, both two- and four-year public colleges have seen greater increases in price in the past ten years. Whether consumers consider sticker price or net price (and even which net price) will determine, to a great extent, which type of institution, public or private, they feel is most affordable.

In an attempt to understand the causes of price increases, the cost commission identified a number of cost drivers, cost drivers that are particularly salient for private colleges that do not have access to state subsidies to offset their impact. The commission examined the potential role that the following cost drivers have in increasing the price of college attendance: (1) financial aid, (2) people, (3) facilities, (4) technology, (5) regulations, and (6) expectations. All six cost drivers warrant serious attention, but we focus on the role of student aid in determining college costs and price. Although the commission expressed concern at the increasing levels of debt that college students were assuming, they found "no evidence to suggest any relationship between the availability of federal grants and the costs or prices of . . . institutions" (National Commission on the Cost of Higher Education, 1998, p. 9). Furthermore, the commission concluded that there is no "conclusive" evidence linking student loans to increased costs, although there appears to be some conflicting empirical evidence in this area. Finally, the commission found "that there is slightly stronger evidence that increases in institutional aid have been one of the cost and price drivers, as institutional aid grew by 178 percent between 1987 and 1996. Since most of the revenue for institutional aid comes from tuition dollars, it seems reasonable to conclude that tuition could have increased slightly less had institutions not been putting these revenues into institutional aid" (National Commission on the Cost of Higher Education, 1998, p. 9).

Similar evidence was found by the U.S. General Accounting Office (1998), which concluded that the two primary cost drivers for public and private schools were increased institutional expenditures (including both instructional and noninstructional costs) and decreased state appropriations and contract and grant revenues.

The evidence is clear. Costs and prices at all the nation's colleges have increased substantially over the past decade. Furthermore, institutional student aid may have contributed to the increased prices students and families must bear. Finally, "confusion about cost and price abounds and the distinction between the two must be recognized and respected" (National Commission on the Cost of Higher Education, 1998, p. 13). These factors will have an impact on who is attracted to a college, whether they can stay once enrolled, and how effectively a college can shape its student body to meet its institutional goals. The following section presents a discussion of the issues of access, institutional choice, and quality and their importance to private colleges.

Access, Choice, and Quality.   American college students benefit from a rich array of student aid programs that have been created to meet a number of important economic, social, and political goals (including the need for a skilled workforce, student quality and diversity objectives, and as rewards for certain citizens). However, the most fundamental goal of student aid has been to provide opportunities to as many people as possible who might benefit from further education and training. This goal has evolved over time, with the most dramatic changes occurring since the end of World War II. With the development of the GI Bill, the federal government, and most colleges, committed to a goal of providing postsecondary education to as many people as possible. The goal of providing access to postsecondary education was further expanded with passage of the National Defense Education Act in 1958 and the Higher Education Act of 1965. In the early 1970s, a second policy goal, student choice, was added to the equation with development of the Basic Educational Opportunity Grant program (currently the Pell Grant program). *Access* suggests that the basic opportunity to pursue further education is a right for every citizen, and *choice* would imply that citizens should be afforded the option to pursue an education that best fits their individual needs and aspirations. At the institutional level, assuring both access and choice must be mediated by other factors, such as costs associated with remediation and counseling for students, the increasing cost of technology, climbing faculty salaries, research support, and facility maintenance. At private colleges all these funding needs are dependent on student enrollment as the primary source of income. Without stable, and perhaps continually growing, enrollment levels, institutional revenue streams will be constrained and realizing the goals of access and choice may be limited.

For private colleges, the policy options of access and choice are further confounded by the need, at least at highly selective colleges, to present an image of quality. In their examination of selective, liberal arts colleges, Duffy and Goldberg (1998) examine the delicate relationship between institutional merit aid and institutional reputation. They note that buying students with large institutional aid awards may send the wrong message to discriminating student applicants. And that message is this: "Why should you go to a college that can only attract the best and the brightest if they have to entice you there with large aid awards." Duffy and Goldberg (1998) characterize the actions of many private colleges that raised tuition significantly in the 1980s as the "Chivas Regal phenomenon." They note that for many colleges, and a large number of parent and student consumers, price is directly linked to quality. In the 1980s, colleges looked very carefully at the relationship of price to perceptions of quality and to peer institutions' tuition and fee charges. Duffy and Goldberg suggest that recent marketing strategies (supported by a new generation of college guides such as those developed by *U.S. News and World Report* and *Money*) promoting colleges as "best buys" may have diminished the Chivas Regal phenomenon. Nevertheless, many selective, and some less selective colleges, carefully consider the impression that low costs send to consumers.

Although private colleges are firmly committed to balancing the goals of equity, choice, and quality, realizing those goals presents interesting and often thorny challenges. The ability of a college to meet those challenges depends on a number of policy decisions that are formalized through the interplay of institutional pricing strategies, merit and tuition discounting, and institutional student aid packaging policies.

Financial Responses to Enrollment Imperatives

Institutions seeking to utilize their financial resources to attract and retain students must carefully consider how they set tuition and fee levels (White and Fishberg, 1977), the amount of institutional funds they allocate for student aid, and how they construct student aid packages. The interplay of these policy decisions will not only have an impact on enrollment but will also have important implications for the financial health of the institution. Perhaps the most important financial decision that institutions must make is determining the amount of institutional financial aid it will fund in a given year, thereby establishing the institution's discount rate.

In explaining the term *discount,* some basic definitions of institutional accounting are needed. Although the focus here is on the private sector, in the 1990s "both public and private institutions have increased institutional financial aid at spectacular real rates" (McPherson and Schapiro, 1998, p. 60). Essential to any discussion of institutional scholarships and grants is the matter of how they are funded. Generally speaking, an institution can "fund" a scholarship from one of three sources: endowment income, annual giving, or tuition. Endowments (that is, gifts to the institution that are invested) provide an income stream that "pays" for the scholarship. The student who has the scholarship does not pay, but the institution still receives the revenue. An endowment often is permanent in nature and ideally appreciates in market value, thus preserving the income it produces against the increased cost of inflation. The annual receipt of a donation to the institution from a benefactor or outside donor organization is the second means of funding institutional scholarships. Funds from donors are expended, not invested; the student does not pay and the institution receives income, but only once. The final and most common source of funding of institutional scholarships, however, is tuition, that is, the money paid by students and their families. Students who receive institutional scholarships or grants funded in this manner do not have to pay the amount of the tuition bill covered by the award, *but* the institution does *not* receive income. The institution simply has reduced the student's bill, calling this discount a "scholarship." This loss of revenue, or "discount," is actually an expense on the cost side of the operating budget. Because expenses are primarily offset by tuition, any increase in these expenses creates an equal increase in the need for tuition revenues. Such "discounting" describes "the familiar pattern of financial aid increases wiping out a good portion of the increase in gross tuition in the private sector" (McPherson and Schapiro, 1998, p. 68). In a very real sense, those students who are paying, sometimes with loans, are helping to fund those who are receiving (tuition funded) scholarships.

Depending on what is included in the institution's numerator (for example, merit aid, athletic grants, employee tuition benefits, room reimbursement for residence hall staff), and the denominator (all revenue; tuition revenue only; tuition and fee revenue only; tuition, fee, room, and board revenue only), a "discount rate" can be determined. Part of the difficulty in understanding this term is the simple fact that, as the cost commission noted, there is not a clear and commonly accepted definition of *discount*. This includes differences of opinion on what exactly should be included as factors in determining the numerator and the denominator. The chief financial officer of the institution may focus narrowly on the tuition revenue not collected, whereas enrollment managers might define it as the amount of tuition the student does not have to pay. These amounts are different because of the role played by institutional and outside grants in the student aid process. This practice, of course, does not discriminate between those who can afford to pay all the tuition versus those who cannot, including those who are borrowing to pay their bills. Tuition discounting raises some interesting institutional budgetary questions and often leads to higher tuition levels. The escalation of an institution's discount factor, or the percentage of tuition used for this purpose, has become an increasingly disturbing concern for many institutions (Jenkins, 1990/1991; Riggs, 1994). If too many students have their tuition discounted, through the receipt of institutionally funded merit awards, the lost revenue could reach a point where the institution is unable to meet its financial obligations. Those who argue for higher discount strategies maintain that the net revenue created by scholarship students who might not otherwise enroll is typically greater than it would otherwise have been. Such rationale would suggest that some tuition revenue is better than none. A tension is thus created between controlling tuition increases for all versus the seemingly endless and ever expanding need to increase the discount rate (Allan, 1999).

Scholarships and grants given without regard to financial need are often referred to as *non-need* or *merit* awards. Duffy and Goldberg (1998) trace the development of merit aid at both the institutional and national level. They note that one of the primary reasons for increasing levels of institutional based merit aid was the need for colleges to use "their limited funds to address institutional priorities of quality and diversity" (p. 208). The use of targeted institutional resources to attract specific applicant groups is supported by a statement made by the Johns Hopkins University executive director of academic services: "The goal of a merit aid program ought to be to attract and enroll students who otherwise would not attend an institution" (Duffy and Goldberg, 1998, p. 208). Merit aid programs have existed for years and have rewarded students for a wide range of talents and abilities, but their use in targeted financial aid packaging has shifted the purpose of such awards. No longer are merit awards seen as a reward for services or potential, but as an important cog in the enrollment management machine. For example, Heller and Laird (1999) note that institutions with considerable flexibility in the use of institutional non-need-based aid were awarding fewer non-need grants and that the size of the grants had increased from the period 1989–1990 to 1995–1996. Furthermore, they note that the "growth in the number of need-based awards was largest among high income students, for whom the number of these awards grew at a rate three times that of low income students" (Heller and Laird, 1999, p. 18.). Although research studies like those of Heller and Laird (1999), Riggs (1994), Schuh (1998), and Somers (1993) help institutional policymakers determine the relative value of merit and non-need-based aid, additional research is warranted. This is particularly necessary in examining the retention dynamics of merit aid recipients.

Linked directly to this new merit aid role are a new set of student aid packaging strategies that have been implemented to help institutions meet enrollment goals (Duffy and Goldberg, 1998). As federal, state, and institutional aid resources have failed to keep pace with rapidly escalating costs, student aid officers and other institutional policymakers are considering the best ways to package scarce institutional resources to attract and retain students. In their examination of the role of student aid in the enrollment management process, Duffy and Goldberg (1998) describe the following types of packaging strategies:

Preferential packaging. This process involves packaging the most desirable student applicant's need-based financial aid awards with more grant and less loan aid. The intent is to recognize academic and other distinctions and reward those distinctions by lowering the net-cost to students.

Differential packaging. These awards are predicated on assumptions more consonant with the original philosophy of need-based student aid. Differential packaging involves "the awarding of more attractive packages to the most needy, rather than the academically strongest students. Although intended to ensure that the most needy students do not graduate with enormous debts, differential packaging policies have also helped colleges attract minority students without explicitly favoring them" (Duffy and Goldberg, 1998, p. 224).

Price-sensitive packaging. Perhaps the most sophisticated and certainly the most controversial, price-sensitive packaging (or financial aid leveraging) is predicated on the assumption that the applicant's desire to attend the institution should determine how the applicant is packaged. Using sophisticated marketing data and econometric models, student aid and admissions officers can project which students are most likely to choose and then enroll at a particular college. Students who are deemed "locks" are awarded smaller packages or packages with higher levels of self-help (thus increasing the net price to the student). Students who are wavering (particularly students from categories the institution has targeted to meet diversity or academic enhancement goals) are awarded packages meeting their full need or packages with a more favorable grant to self-help ratio.

Two unintended outcomes of the "leveraging" (Noya, 1997) of institutional student aid resources to shape an institution's enrollment picture have been the rise of financial aid consultants and the changed perception on the part of student aid consumers that financial aid awards are negotiable (Mumper, 1999). A growing cadre of financial aid consultants is now assisting colleges in targeting their aid awards to optimize enrollment goals (Gose, 1999). Financial aid consultants may be providing valuable research and analytical expertise that many colleges do not possess, but they may also be adding to the perception that the primary goals of student aid are not aiding needy students, but filling campus classrooms and residence halls. However, colleges are not alone. Many students and families are turning to consultants to assist them in the preparation of student aid applications and in the shaping of family financial resources to optimize student need. In addition, students and families are considering the higher education arena an open market and forcing colleges to engage in "bidding wars." Some institutions, in an attempt to enroll certain students identified as highly desirable within their enrollment goals, have taken to publishing in their admissions literature statements that they are prepared to match any other institution's student aid offer. This coupled with applicants' desire to secure the most favorable student aid package has led to a more open, but perhaps less equitable, student aid system.

Structural Responses to Enrollment Imperatives

In order to respond to new enrollment imperatives, colleges have reorganized themselves. Colleges have had to modify their institutional structures by realigning functional relationships and by creating new administrative positions like that of the enrollment manager. The importance of this new role is evidenced by according it the administrative title of dean or vice president and often providing it with direct reporting responsibilities to the institution's chief executive officer. The responsibilities of this function include institutional efforts to recruit (admissions, marketing, publications, Web sites), retain (registrar, counseling), graduate, and out-place students. In addition, because enrollment is linked more than ever with meeting the fiscal needs of the institution, enrollment managers are also involved in projecting revenue and expenditures in the annual budget review process.

The application of enrollment management concepts to the operation of student financial aid has resulted in a new delivery model—the *student financial services* approach. This emerging approach integrates enrollment management goals, a customer service orientation (Lackey and Pugh, 1994), and the development of new products that provide students with a more affordable means of fee payment. Institutions employing this model seek a more cooperative spirit between the financial aid office and those offices responsible for the billing and collection of student fees, such as the bursars or student accounts offices.

For example, the University of Notre Dame has chosen to take the student financial services approach. Because the enrollment side had strong leadership and a solid applicant pool boosted by an increasingly positive national reputation, yet had a significant need to improve its reputation for inadequate scholarship assistance, the student financial services model was developed. A newly energized financial aid office and new leadership in the student accounts office were realigned to report to the same university administrator, the assistant vice president for planning and budget. Much improved communications in assisting students and families and providing service has effectively changed the culture and reputation of both offices. The recognition of the need for new products and services to help families from all income levels has resulted in the creation of perhaps the most competitive array of payment options available to college students. And as a result of all of these changes, the cash flow to the institution has improved dramatically. From the enrollment management perspective, all these changes have contributed to a major improvement in the quality and diversity of the student body. Together they have added even more to the institution's national reputation. One of the desirable consequences often expected of an enhanced spirit of cooperation is improved cash flow for the institution. Improved cash flow helps meet budget needs and temper the need for tuition increases, thereby offsetting the need for more institutional aid. Tuition discounting is frequently seen as a way of enhancing enrollments and attracting new sources of revenue for a college; however, implementing structural changes that emphasize increased organizational efficiency may accomplish the same goals with less direct cost to the institution.

Future Issues

Although we have focused primarily on private institutions, many of the issues are applicable to the public sector as well. Reduced public subsidies for higher education, and their impact on the amount of tuition students will be required to pay, appear to be a continuing trend. Though access may still be provided, it may indeed become more limited, effectively restricting enrollment at competitive, flagship public institutions to the most qualified and generally to the more affluent applicants. The need to diversify the student body may prompt more public institutions to employ sophisticated enrollment management strategies in the future.

The cost of these strategies, particularly in terms of the discount issues raised above, may be the single most critical factor in shaping the future of such policies. In the private sector, the growing concern for the discount factor is often discussed by institutional governing boards. The major and escalating expense resulting from "bidding wars" employing merit-based aid will increase concerns about the relationship of discount rates to institutional costs—concerns that may have many colleges rethinking their enrollment strategies.

Ethical issues must also be considered. For example, admissions offices must consider whether the needs and goals of a recruited student might truly be well served by enrolling at a particular institution. Research on the effectiveness of merit aid in recruiting students is mixed at best (Wick, 1997), and further research is needed.

Other less public, yet difficult, issues are worthy of further review. Some colleges are aggressively using price-sensitive packaging to realize enrollment goals. Basing the decision to accept a student on that student's ability to pay, versus the applicant's academic potential to succeed, challenges the traditional student aid policy of assuring access and opportunity. However, such policies are defended on the basis of fairness to the student (whose need, perhaps, was not going to be met anyway), as well as by the broader enrollment needs and budget constraints of the institution. These practices suggest that an institution is no longer "need-blind" in its admissions policies. Such practices need to be examined carefully from both the perspective of the student and the institution.

Conclusion

The basic goals of access and opportunity will continue to be pulled in the opposite direction by rising college costs. Policymakers in government and at institutional levels cannot ignore the clear trend toward reducing public subsidies. Nor can they continue to increase discount rates at the expense of needy students in order to fund merit scholarships for able students who will certainly be successful regardless of whether such awards are made.

New and creative ways for helping make college more affordable must be developed. State governments need to craft policy that puts the funding of education as a major priority. Federal policymakers also need to review carefully their funding priorities, their thinking on tax policies, and the tendencies to impose very expensive and burdensome regulations on institutions—regulations that ultimately are paid for by students. More emphasis needs to be placed on providing incentives for families to plan and save for college. Institutions need to revisit their original missions, become more efficient in managing their resources and budgets, control tuition increases, develop new revenue streams, and look seriously at their discount rates and what is driving them. Professional associations of institutional administrators need to reaffirm a code of good practices and ethics that will effectively guide program and policy development. A major overhaul of the current need analysis methodology would also be helpful. Such a transformation would be especially useful if it could combine much needed incentives (rather than the current disincentives) for college savings with updated economic assumptions about how the family's ability to pay is measured. These changes will require careful balancing of reasonable allowances for the current expenditures needed to maintain a moderate standard of living against those which would serve to foster unnecessary consumption and lifestyle choices by families.

The private sector also needs to step up. Philanthropic and community organizations and employers need to expand their funding of scholarships and other forms of student assistance. Employers should develop simple payroll deduction mechanisms that encourage employees to set aside money for college. Those funds might be matched by the employer after a predetermined period of employment. Such savings and matching plans should be supported by the federal and state governments through the exemption of some or all of these contributions from taxation. Employers should also consider expanding current education benefits provided for employees by creating new programs that would assist employees in repaying student loans. This idea would not only serve as a recruitment incentive but might also enhance employee retention.

Perhaps as important as any strategy is the need to better educate everyone in appreciating the real value of education. All educators need to do a more effective job of explaining the individual and societal benefits that flow from a more educated citizenry.

In the final analysis, perhaps the most basic of questions for policymakers at the government and especially at the institutional level will be, Should policies dictate resources or should resources dictate policies? Any successful organization will balance this basic question properly. The long-term pricing strategy for any institution must be sensitive to the institution's basic mission, its marketplace position, and its need to be fiscally responsible. Once this kind of vision is properly framed, the annual budget process, including enrollment strategy and tuition increases, would seem to have a more properly determined and solidly balanced future.

References

Allan, R. G. "A Taxonomy of Tuition Discounting." *Journal of Student Financial Aid,* 1999, 29 (2), 7–20.

Clotfelter, C. *Buying the Best: Cost Escalation in Elite Higher Education.* Princeton, N.J.: Princeton University Press, 1996.

College Board. *Trends in College Pricing, 1998.* Washington, D.C.: College Board, 1998.

Duffy, E. A., and Goldberg, I. *Crafting a Class: College Admissions and Financial Aid, 1955–1994.* Princeton, N.J.: Princeton University Press, 1998.

Gose, B. "Colleges Turn to Consultants to Shape the Freshman Class." *Chronicle of Higher Education,* May 7, 1999, pp. A46, A51, A52.

Heller, D. E., and Laird, T. F. N. "Institutional Use of Need and Non-Need Financial Aid: What Can We Learn from NPSAS?" Paper presented at the 16th annual Research Network Conference sponsored by the National Association of State Student Grant and Aid Programs and the National Council for Higher Education Loan Programs, Savannah, Ga., May 1999.

Jenkins, R. E. "The Dangers of Current Tuition Strategies," *Student Aid Transcript,* 1990, 3 (3), 4–7.

Lackey, C. W., and Pugh, S. L. "With TQM Less Is More for Students." *Student Aid Transcript,* 1994, 6 (2), 7–11.

McPherson, M. S., and Schapiro, M. O. *The Student Aid Game: Meeting Need and Rewarding Talent in American Higher Education.* Princeton, N.J.: Princeton University Press, 1998.

Mumper, M. "The Student Aid Industry." In J. E. King (ed.), *Financing a College Education: How It Works, How It's Changing.* Phoenix: Oryx Press, 1999.

National Commission on the Cost of Higher Education. *Straight Talk About College Costs and Prices.* Phoenix: Oryx Press, 1998.

Noya, R. "Financial Aid Leveraging in Higher Education: How Is It Done, Is It Fair, and What Is Its Role in the '90s?" *On Target,* Spring 1997, pp. 19–23.

Riggs, H. E. "Are Merit Scholarships Threatening the Future of Private Colleges?" *Trusteeship,* May–June 1994, pp. 6–10.

Schuh, J. H. "Measuring the Cost Effectiveness of Financial Aid from an Institutional Perspective: A Case Study." Paper presented at the annual meeting of the National Association of Student Personnel Administrators, Philadelphia, March 1998.

Somers, P. "Are 'Mondo' Scholarships Effective?" *Journal of Student Financial Aid,* 1993, 23 (2), 37–38.

U.S. General Accounting Office. *Higher Education: Tuition Increases and Colleges' Efforts to Contain Costs* (GAU/HEHS-98-227). Washington, D.C.: U.S. General Accounting Office, 1998.

Vogelstein, F. "Paying for College: How High Can Tuition Go?" *U.S. News and World Report,* Sept. 7, 1998. 125 (9), 68–70.

White, P., and Fishberg, E. "Why Money Drives the Private College Admissions Process." *Student Aid Transcript,* 1977, 8 (3), 32–34.

Wick, P. G. *No-Need/Merit Scholarships: Practices and Trends, 1943–Present.* New York: College Board, 1997.

JOSEPH A. RUSSO is director of financial aid at the University of Notre Dame and editor of the Journal of Student Financial Aid.

MICHAEL D. COOMES is associate professor of higher education and student affairs and chair of the college student personnel program at Bowling Green State University.

4

A shift in government policy and changing demographics have forced college students to seek alternative ways of paying for college. This chapter explores the various strategies used by students and the impact they can have on students' success.

Alternative Financing Methods for College

Robert DeBard

In helping college students of today meet their educational expenses, financial aid officers have come to realize that institutional capability has been overwhelmed by individual need. The increasing difficulty of providing aid packages sufficient to meet expenses has been made even more complex because students bring a greater diversity of motivation for attendance, expectation of attendance, and academic preparation level than ever before. The result is a need not only for students to seek alternative methods of financing for college, but also an inclination on the part of students to do so.

This chapter discusses the pressure on students to seek alternatives, explores the student as a worker in college, and then presents strategies that have been effective in helping students meet their financial obligations. Some mention is made as to how families are adapting to government policy that encourages new ways of saving for college, although institutional and government policy is dealt with more adequately elsewhere in this volume. It is the diversity of attendance that has added to the complexity of financial need. In 1995, whereas a majority of traditional age undergraduate students (eighteen to twenty-four years of age) still attended on a full-time basis (62.6 percent), more than four out of ten of all undergraduate students attended on a part-time basis (41.6 percent). Close to two out of three of these students (63.3 percent) were of nontraditional age (National Center for Education Statistics, 1997). This realization suggests that financial aid professionals who would help these students meet their obligations must realize that alternative financing strategies must accommodate a new time and a new clientele.

The Pressure to Seek Alternatives

Consider the data that indicate the challenge of paying for a college education. From 1981 to 1994, the cost of attending a public university rose 153
percent; it rose 203 percent at private universities. This was at the same time
that the median family income rose by only 75 percent (Gladieux and
Knapp, 1994). Between 1977 and 1995 costs at four-year public colleges
represented an increase from 12.7 percent of median family income to 17.3
percent. The percentage of family income required at four-year private colleges increased even more dramatically from 34.4 percent in 1987 to 43.3
percent in 1995 (Davis, 1997).

These increases have been felt most acutely by those least able to afford
them. The U.S. Department of Commerce report *School Enrollment: Social
and Economic Characteristics of Students* (1993) observes that college-age
young people from the highest income range (over $75,000) are over three
times more likely to be enrolled in college than those from the lowest
income groups (under $15,000). Aside from what might be considered the
traditional disparity of economic class, the situation is getting worse.
Attending a public four-year college or university costs 62 percent of a low-
income family's income and 17 percent of a middle-income family's income
(Gladieux and Hauptman, 1995). Kane (1995) reports that the gap in
enrollment rates for students from families in the lowest income quartile
and students from the more affluent families grew by 12 percentage points
between 1980 and 1993. Research shows that students from middle-low-
income families are much more price sensitive than students from middle-
upper-income families (McPherson and Schapiro, 1991; St. John, 1994).
According to Orfield (1992), minority and low-income access is declining
because upper-middle-income political power has helped sway policy in the
1990s: "The most fundamental assumptions about who attends college,
what makes attendance possible, and who should be helped are suddenly
being challenged, under the pressure by parents frightened by the burden
of soaring tuition and fees and politicians seeking their votes" (p. 337).

This creation of greater burden on the part of students has occurred at
a time when the financial benefits to be accrued from a college education
have never been greater. In 1996, a male with a bachelor's degree or higher
earned 54 percent more than males who had a high school diploma, whereas
women earned 88 percent more than their high school educated counter-
parts (National Center for Education Statistics, 1999). McPherson and
Schapiro (1991) agree that higher lifetime earnings for college graduates
provide substantial incentive to enroll despite rising costs.

The pressure to attend converging with the pressure to pay has been
exacerbated by shifts in government funding policy that force students and
their families to seek alternative funding strategies. Davis (1997) reports
that between 1984 and 1993, 78 percent of the growth in net tuition was the

result of shifting larger shares of the costs to students when financial support from state government and other sources diminished. Part of the reason for this shift in policy is simply the limitations of public expenditure. "The public share of total enrollment cannot expand much further. Postsecondary enrollments have grown so large that expanding the total government subsidy per student has become a very expensive proposition" (McPherson and Schapiro, 1991).

Any discussion of government subsidy must begin with the role of the federal government. Federal funding represented 75 percent of the close to $42 billion in total financial aid assistance to students in 1993 (National Association of Student Financial Affairs Officers, 1995). Today, loans have become the primary source of aid to students. Since the 1970s, loans have increased from about one-fifth to more than half of all student aid (Gladieux and Hauptman, 1995). At the federal level, loans increased from 39 percent of federal aid in 1970–1971 to 65 percent of aid in 1990–1991 (Knapp, 1992). Student loan indebtedness increased almost three times faster than college costs and four times faster than family incomes (Merisotis and Parker, 1996). Whereas in 1976, 21 percent of total federal grants and loans aid packages were made up of loans, by 1994, 72 percent were loans (Gladieux and Knapp, 1994). The philosophical bottom line is that the issue of who benefits and who should pay for higher education has shifted: "Higher education has come to be seen by the federal government as an individual good, a means for students to help themselves, rather than as a societal good" (Kurz, 1995, p. 27).

As loans have displaced grant dollars, students from various income levels have been affected differently. According to St. John (1994), increased borrowing has adversely affected retention for low-income students while actually increasing educational choice for middle-income families. Campaigne and Hossler (1998) state, "It is well documented that there are significant differences in the willingness of students and their families of diverse levels to take out loans. Families and students from lower income groups are more adverse to taking out loans" (p. 92). The General Accounting Office confirmed this in its report *Restructuring Student Aid Could Reduce Low-Income College Student Dropouts* (1995) by indicating that a $1,000 increase in loan aid means a 3 percent increase in student dropout rates, whereas a $1,000 increase in grant aid means a 14 percent decrease in dropout rates. In a comprehensive analysis of the decline in the college attendance of African Americans, Hauser (1992) concludes that African Americans were less willing to borrow for higher education because they have doubts about the benefits. "A student's willingness to borrow will be affected by the economic return to his or her investment" (p. 302). So students in general and low-income and nontraditional students in particular have had to seek alternatives to indebtedness. The next section of this chapter considers the primary means students have chosen to finance their higher education.

The Student as a Worker

The National Center for Education Statistics' report *Postsecondary Financing Strategies: How Undergraduates Combine Work, Borrowing, and Attendance* (1998) indicates that close to three out of four undergraduate students work while enrolled in higher education. Even more provocatively, however, the report found that students do so for close to 90 percent of the time they are in college and for an average of 31 hours per week. The report also found the percentage of full-time college students aged sixteen to twenty-four who worked increased from 34 percent in 1970 to 47 percent in 1995. It is interesting that "most of the rise in employment among college students as a whole is attributable to growing employment among four-year college students" (Stern and Nakata, 1991, p. 30). During the 1992–1993 academic year, students attending exclusively part-time became the largest plurality (43 percent) of undergraduates in higher education whereas the number enrolling exclusively full-time was 41 percent. Fully two-thirds of two-year college students enrolled part-time, and eight out of ten of these worked; close to half worked more than 34 hours per week. This movement in attendance patterns is not surprising since, "in an era of reduced financial aid, some students will be forced to work more and study less. . . . research showed that financially needy students often dropped out, changed from four-year to two-year institutions or shifted to part-time status" (Orfield, 1992, p. 342).

Also, there has been a fundamental shift in the demographics of college attendees that has resulted in an emphasis on work as a financing alternative in paying for college. A larger proportion of students now commute, work while in college, and study part-time (Baker and Velez, 1996). The National Center for Education Statistics (1998) reports that between 1970 and 1994, the part-time fall enrollment in higher education more than doubled whereas full-time enrollment rose 40 percent.

A major problem regarding public policy related to these changing student demographics is that the philosophy that students will borrow to invest in their future earnings does not necessary hold. As age increases, the likelihood of attending exclusively part-time increases from 24 percent for those less than age twenty-four to 73 percent for those over thirty. Currently, close to one-third of female undergraduates are over age thirty (National Center for Education Statistics, 1998). Significantly, 90 percent of part-time students do not borrow at all and only 5 percent of two-year college students borrow. This compares to 23 percent of four-year public and 34 percent of four-year private students who borrow (National Center for Education Statistics, 1998).

The attendance patterns of part-time students could be reconciled under the banner of student choice if it were not for the fact that these patterns result in very different levels of academic success. Students who attend full-time are far more likely to persist (73 percent) than those who attend part-time (25 percent), and these statistics hold for all types of institutions (National Center for Education Statistics, 1998). The evidence is reasonably consistent that employment off-campus has a negative influence on both year to year persistence in college and completion of a bachelor's degree (Pascarella and Terenzini, 1991; Bean and Metzner, 1985). In an opinion piece appearing in the *Chronicle of Higher Education,* Jacqueline King (1998) notes that "much has been said and written about student indebtedness, yet the more serious problem may be that students are working long hours to eliminate or at least lessen their need to borrow and in the process, imperiling their ability to succeed academically" (p. A72).

It is the number of hours per week of employment that has the deleterious impact on student success. For nonborrowers, the likelihood of persistence decreases with each increase in average hours worked—from 80 percent for those who work one to fourteen hours, and 61 percent for those who work fifteen to thirty-three hours, to 25 percent for those who work thirty-four or more hours per week (National Center for Education Statistics, 1998). The point is that it is not work that is the problem, but the extent of work. In the mid-1980s, Astin (1985) found that although part-time work shows some negative influence, the consequences become substantially more deleterious when off-campus employment increases to full-time. Other studies have found some evidence that limited working need not adversely affect academic success (Ehrenberg and Sherman, 1987; Hammes and Haller, 1983). It has long been accepted that limited employment on campus can actually help persistence and academic achievement (Pascarella and Terenzini, 1991). But when working becomes more dominant than studying, persistence becomes an issue.

When students balance borrowing with limited part-time work, preferably on-campus, the results have been shown to be beneficial. "Among students at four-year institutions working similar numbers of hours, borrowers were generally more likely than nonborrowers to attend full time" (National Center for Education Statistics, 1998, p. 23). As previously cited, students who attend full-time are far more likely to persist than part-time students. King cites longitudinal research conducted by the National Center for Education Statistics (NCES) in supporting her premise that working fewer than fifteen hours can have a positive effect on the likelihood of staying in college whereas working more has a negative effect. She suggests, "Campus officials must help students understand that it may be to their best interest to borrow, so that they can work fewer hours" (p. A72). George Vaughan, when he was a community college president in the 1980s, asserted, "We always talked about the foregone income of going to college. What we should be doing with our students is calculating the foregone earnings of going to school part-time and thereby delaying receiving a degree and higher earnings that can be commanded" (McCartan, 1988, p. 17).

As research shows, however, working during college is the common practice of students, so the question becomes how best to make work an effective strategy that allows students to attain their educational aspirations. The next section of this chapter reviews policies, programs, and professional orientation, beyond the grants and loans associated with financial aid, that can be utilized to help students finance higher education.

Employment Strategies That Work

The extent students work in college can be seen as a barometer of their commitment to achieve their educational aspirations. Students who hold full-time jobs do not have lower aspirations than those who do not work or who limit their work so as not to interfere with their educational goals; employment creates a pressure that interacts with other pressures, including academic rigor, in a student's life. If well balanced, these pressures can actually form a synergy of challenge and support, but if work becomes too intrusive the result can be educational aspiration deferred. "The tension between working and learning might best be viewed along a continuum reflecting what students perceive as their primary affiliation or commitment. The continuum has less to do with hours worked or credits pursued than the level of personal or professional involvement at work or at college, motivation to pursue a degree, and the sense by a student as to where his or her primary responsibility lies" (McCartan, 1988, p. 12).

Another way of looking at what drives student decision about whether to work, the extent of work, where to attend, and the extent of the attendance has been offered by Paulsen and St. John (1997): "The heart of the financial nexus is based on interactions between students' prematriculation expectations about financial factors that influence choice and their post-matriculation financial experience and the way this interaction influences persistence" (p. 68). Despite the fact that students might have the best of intentions in pursuing their education, Paulsen and St. John (1997) found that financial factors were significant in the choice of college and that the choice of "could work" was second only to "low tuition" as very important in students' choice of college.

Given that the majority of students are going to work and a growing plurality are choosing to pursue their education part-time and also that although student loans are now the most common form of student aid, a minority of total students are choosing to borrow through student loan programs, provision should be made to give greater attention to helping make work an effective strategy for financing higher education. There is a need for those who would help today's college students pursue higher education to view student employment as a necessary component rather than an optional augmentation. The Task Force on General Education of the American Association of Colleges report titled *A New Vitality in General Education* (Katz, 1988) comments that a significant amount of student time is taken up by paid jobs, but integration of this work experience into the classroom has been rare.

Still, the need to make meaningful connection between work and school has been advanced by researchers and demonstrated by institutions. McCartan (1988) cites Kenneth Green of UCLA's Higher Education Research Institute, who speculates that students work as much to get a jump on the job market as to meet expenses, and William Ramsay of the National Association of Student Employment Administrators, who has witnessed a growing involvement of career services officers in helping the quality of student work through job location and development.

A number of institutions have purposefully linked schooling with work. Scannell and Simpson (1996) provide a comprehensive overview of where work has been merged with experiential education for the benefit of students. Among the programs cited, the Cornell Tradition, Duke Futures, the Dana Foundation Student Aid for Educational Quality, and Reach for Rochester are all credited with meeting several goals, including the development of individual self-worth on the part of students, successful recruitment strategies for institutions, the creation of connections with alumni and alumnae, the chance to engage employers, the opportunity to involve faculty in research with students to address large scale social, economic and environmental challenges, and the development of external support for students and the institution. Furthermore, they found that these programs helped students affirm their career plans more than change them, and although there was no evidence that these experiences have a positive value on one's academic performance, there was evidence of the development of greater civic responsibility and a sense of self-confidence.

The need to link meaningful work with academic programs has been advanced as a strategy to add educational quality. Lovett (1995), in an opinion piece in the *Chronicle of Higher Education,* discusses the new ideas that need to emerge to improve higher education in the face of greater state and federal scrutiny by suggesting, "Given that most students are employed, why not make employment on campus an integral part of the undergraduate experience, perhaps even as a requirement for graduation" (p. B3). There is little prospect of such a requirement, but the premise that work and learning can be merged is clearly a viable alternative strategy for funding higher education as long as institutions are dedicated to turning this experiential education into intentional educational outcomes.

One national program that has had significant impact on student earnings while incorporating experiential learning is cooperative education. Estimates are that close to 250,000 students from more than one thousand colleges and universities are participating in formal cooperative education programs (Van Gyn, 1997). Cooperative education has linked the classroom with the workplace through formal program options that vary in the amount of work obligation, academic credits earned while working, and level of pay. Engineering programs at the university level have been the predominant area, but the greatest growth in recent years has been within two-year programs at community colleges. "Career development is a major objective of community college students, and programs to promote it need to be a major priority of community colleges" (Healy and Mourton, 1987, p. 28). Community colleges now account for close to half of cooperative education programs around the country. La Guardia Community College now requires a co-op experience; Lane County Community College has more than two thousand, or two out of every three, students involved. It has been advanced that the co-op work experience in community colleges has a positive impact on the career development of students, as well as establishing a sense of purpose and life style planning (Trach and Harney, 1998). Stan Patterson, program specialist for cooperative education with the Department of Education, provides some meaningful figures that help demonstrate the viability of cooperative education: "In 1986, co-op students earned nearly $2 billion and they paid more than $250 million in taxes and Social Security. That's quite a return on the $14 million that the federal government spent on these programs" (Stanton, 1988, p. 25).

Programs such as cooperative education are viable for certain academic disciplines; however, they require significant institutional investment in administrative support. A more promising approach would be the significant expansion of federal work-study programs that have proven to be effective in helping those with demonstrable need gain access to higher education and succeed within it. James Mingle, executive director of the State Higher Education Officers (SHEEO), reports "a positive relationship between work-study and both retention and academic performance" (Hauptman and Koff, 1991, p. 162). The problem is that both federal and state-based work-study programs have been limited to students from low-income families. This simply does not take into consideration the reality of current student demographics that have fewer than six of every ten full-time students declared as dependents while just over one in five part-time students are considered dependent for financial aid purposes (National Center for Education Statistics, 1998). A report from the Institute for Higher Education Policy recommends a modification of the federal work-study program to expand opportunities for student work that are related in a meaningful way to declared educational and career goals. "Broadened employment options would result in increased student satisfaction with their collegiate experience and therefore the likelihood of uninterrupted persistence" (Merisotis, 1997, p. 40). Such an expansion could well address the concerns of federal officials who wish to assign responsibility to students whom they feel benefit most from a college education and should invest themselves in paying for it (Linsley, 1997). It could also place reasonable limits on the extent of student work that otherwise can adversely affect student success (King, 1998).

If any such system is truly to address the concerns raised in this chapter, a willingness to combine strategies is necessary. Here is where students need the help of professionals who are capable of combining financial and career planning. "Increasingly we should conceptualize the introductory process of career development as combining a first, preemployment stage with a structured, part-time supplement to be pursued during the first years on the job" (Lynton, 1989, p. 32). Unfortunately, more than nine out of ten students work off-campus an average of 31 hours per week (National Center for Education Statistics, 1998). As long as employment is seen strictly as a financial option, students will be left to their own devices. Financial need should be coupled with educational programming if the potential benefit of employment as a funding strategy is to be fully realized.

Tax Incentives as a Strategy

It is clear that work programs must be balanced with other alternative strategies for financing a higher education. Certainly creating tax incentives represents a major method for providing educational opportunity. One of the most promising programs under section 127 of the tax code allows employers to support the educational expenses of their employees. Unfortunately, in 1994, only 10 percent of eligible employees took advantage of this assistance (Merisotis, 1997). Using tax deductions as a method of incentive has proven ineffectual for low-income students because only 9 percent of those who make, or have families who make, under $30,000 itemize (Merisotis, 1997).

A bold new concept advanced by the Clinton administration has been the use of tax credits rather than deductions. The Hope Scholarship and Lifetime Learning tax credits were introduced under the Taxpayer Relief Act of 1997. College freshmen and sophomores and their families are able to claim 100 percent of the first $1,000 a student spends on tuition and fees and 50 percent of the next $1,000 spent. The Lifelong Learning Program allows a tax credit worth 20 percent of the first $5,000 of college costs incurred by part-time students, full-time undergraduates in their third or fourth year, and graduate students. It is estimated that the Hope Scholarship will cost $40 billion over the first five years and $94 billion over ten years (Lederman, 1997).

This legislation is not without controversy. It has been criticized as an incentive to postsecondary institutions to raise their prices. It has also been attacked as a benefit for middle- and upper-income families while not benefiting disadvantaged families with no income tax liability (Saxton and Knight, 1997). The reality is that this legislation was part of an election-year compromise in which tax credits limited to low-income brackets were seen as not palatable to middle-income taxpayers who feel that college costs have outstripped their ability to meet expenses (Orfield, 1992).

Another concern, as with any new federally sponsored financial aid program, has been the institutions' fear of the potential paperwork and need to collect and provide student information. It was reported as of January, 1999 (Hebel, 1999) that final guidelines were still being formulated. The interim rules do not tell institutions how to handle new reporting requirements that they must follow as the new credits take effect. Still, despite the potential for additional administrative work as well as the criticism that the wealthy are being helped more than the poor, the consensus is that the $40 billion in tax breaks is popular with the public (Lederman, 1997).

Expanded IRAs and Other Savings Incentives

Most incentive plans still seem to favor families capable of saving for their children's college. In 1988, the Series EE savings bonds were created to allow interest earned to be exempt from federal tax if used for educational expenses. State-based savings plans were in force in twenty-five states by 1997, and another twenty-one states are contemplating them. Most of these programs involve prepaid tuition plans as a hedge against inflation and as a structured way of putting away money for college. As attractive as such options are, they are based on the assumption that families have enough discretionary money to save for college and are willing to do so as opposed to taking other investment opportunities. In Ohio and Alabama, 60 percent of the users of the prepaid college savings plan come from families with an income over $50,000, but only 20 percent of these states' population are from this income bracket. Of the 33 percent of the states' populations making below $20,000, only 2 percent participated (Merisotis, 1997).

It has been pointed out that the current financial aid system may discourage parents from saving for education because a family's savings can reduce a student's eligibility for grants and scholarships (Saxton and Knight, 1997). The Balanced Budget Act of 1997 includes several incentives aimed at increasing private savings for education. The new law doubles the income limits for which tax-deductible contributions to IRAs are phased out, thereby making these saving plans available to more middle-income families. Penalty-free withdrawals will be allowed for higher education expenses.

There are several economic benefits of IRAs that can be used to support the expenses of higher education. Aside from the obvious ability to deduct IRAs from income and to defer taxes until such time as a family's marginal tax rate may be lower, IRA investments can yield higher returns than tax-free investments (Saxton and Knight, 1997). Additionally, IRAs can promote economic growth through the investment of the savings. The theory holds that the greater capacity of the educational consumer to use savings instead of loans will have a two-fold benefit. First, reduced reliance on student loans can lower government costs, thus allowing the savings to be diverted to federal grants for the poor. Second, expanded IRAs can restore price competition to the marketplace for higher education and provide colleges with incentives to contain tuition while improving quality (Saxton and Knight, 1997). The truth probably would temper this optimism. The wealthy are in position to save and they also have some control of the marketplace. A review of the changing demographics of who is attending higher education suggests that enfranchisement of the poor is more of an issue than empowerment of the rich.

Conclusion

The conclusion drawn is that there cannot be one alternative financing strategy, but rather a matrix of opportunity put together by and for students in a sophisticated way. The responsibility for determining strategy needs to be a partnership between the financial aid professional who represents an institution wishing to recruit students and the individuals who hope to achieve their educational aspirations. "As they take on these new roles, aid officers should adopt a total quality management approach to management, incorporating attention to their customers, effective teamwork, management by fact, planning, and continuous quality improvement" (Kurz, 1995, p. 39). Students need to be provided the necessary information about alternatives and the research findings related to the implementation of various strategies in terms of educational outcomes. They need counsel that takes them into account as individuals needing to be developed rather than simply processed.

This dearth of information about funding alternatives being provided to students also explains why there has been little mention of the use of scholarships and the potential benefit of "consultants" as a strategy for financing higher education. Certainly there are need-based and criteria-based scholarships not being fully tapped by potential recipients. To suggest that the answer is to pay a consultant a finder's fee is a bit like suggesting to taxpayers strapped for cash that they hire a tax consultant to help them out. Would that they could, but if they could afford one they probably would not be strapped for cash. A better answer has been suggested by Cronin (1991) when he describes two cities, Cleveland and Boston, that have made significant progress in encouraging inner-city youth to attend college. In analyzing their success, he found that in both instances, students need not only money but also detailed advice on how to apply for college and qualify for financial aid of any type. It was only after the programs in both cities built an extensive network of caring by those who knew how to maneuver within the system on behalf of those who would otherwise avoid the system that significant progress was made. Professionalism in financial aid will increasingly be defined by the ability to help those needing alternative financing methods to discover what they may be rather than to make decisions based on what the students assume they must be.

References

Astin, A. W. *Achieving Educational Excellence: A Critical Assessment of Priorities and Practices in Higher Education.* San Francisco: Jossey-Bass, 1985.

Baker, T. L., and Velez, W. "Access to Opportunity in Postsecondary Education in the United States: A Review." *Sociology of Education,* 1996 (special issue), 82–101.

Bean, J., and Metzner, B. "A Conceptual Model of Nontraditional Undergraduate Attrition." *Review of Educational Research,* 1985, *55,* 485–540.

Campaigne, D. A., and Hossler, D. "How Do Loans Affect the Educational Decisions of Students? Access, Aspirations, College Choice, and Persistence." In R. Fossey and M.

Bateman (eds.), *Condemning Students to Debt: College Loans and Public Policy.* New York: Teachers College Press, 1998.

Cronin, J. M. "Corporate Support for Scholarships: A Tale of Two Cities." In A. M. Hauptman and R. H. Koff, *New Ways of Paying for College.* New York: American Council of Education/Macmillan, 1991.

Davis, J. S. *College Affordability: A Closer Look at the Crisis.* Washington, D.C.: Sallie Mae Education Institute, 1997.

Ehrenberg, R., and Sherman D. "Employment While in College: Academic and Postcollege Outcomes." *Journal of Human Resources,* 1987, *22,* 1–21.

Gladieux, L. E., and Hauptman, A. M. *The College Aid Quandary: Access, Quality, and the Federal Role.* Washington, D.C.: Brookings Institution, 1995.

Gladieux, L. E., and Knapp, L. G. *Trends in Student Aid, 1984 to 1994.* New York: College Board, 1994.

Hammes, J. F., and Haller, E. J. "Making Ends Meet: Some Consequences of Part-Time Work for College Students." *Journal of College Student Personnel,* 1983, *24,* 529–535.

Hauptman, A. M., and Koff, R. H. *New Ways of Paying for College.* New York: American Council of Education/Macmillan, 1991.

Hauser, R. M. "The Decline in College Entry Among African Americans: Findings in Search of a Meaning." In P. Sniderman, P. Terlock, and E. Carmines (eds.), *Prejudice, Politics, and Race in America Today.* Stanford, Calif.: Stanford University Press, 1992.

Healy, C. C., and Mourton, D. L. "The Relationship of Career Exploration, College Jobs, and Grade Point Average." *Journal of College Student Personnel,* 1987, *28,* 28–33.

Hebel, S. "U.S. Proposes Regulations for People Claiming New Tuition Tax Credits," *Chronicle of Higher Education,* Jan. 15, 1999, p. A34.

Kane, T. J. *Rising Public College Tuition and College Entry: How Well Do Public Subsidies Promote Access to College?* Washington, D.C.: National Bureau of Economic Research, 1995.

Katz, J. *A New Vitality in General Education.* Washington, D.C.: American Association of Colleges, 1998.

King, J. A. "Too Many Students Are Holding Jobs for Too Many Hours." *Chronicle of Higher Education,* May 1, 1998, p. A72.

Knapp, L. G. *Borrowing for College in 1989–90.* Washington, D.C.: College Board, 1992.

Kurz, K. A. "The Changing Role of Financial Aid and Enrollment Management." In R. R. Dixon (ed.), *Making Enrollment Management Work.* New Directions for Student Services, no. 71. San Francisco: Jossey-Bass, 1995.

Lederman, D. "Politicking and Policy Making Behind a $40-Billion Windfall." *Chronicle of Higher Education,* Nov. 28, 1997, p. A28.

Linsley, C. B. "The Underpinnings of Financial Aid." In R. Voorhees (ed.), *Researching Student Aid: Creating an Action Agenda.* New Directions for Institutional Research, no. 95. San Francisco: Jossey-Bass, 1997.

Lovett, C. M. "Small Steps to Achieve Big Changes." *Chronicle of Higher Education,* Nov. 24, 1995, pp. B1–B3.

Lynton, E. A. "Openness and Opportunity." In D. T. Seymour (ed.), *Maximizing Opportunities Through External Relationships.* New Directions for Higher Education, no. 68. San Francisco: Jossey-Bass, 1989.

McCartan, A. M. "Students Who Work: Are They Paying Too High a Price?" *Change,* 1988, *20* (5), 11–20.

McPherson, M. S., and Schapiro, M. O. *Keeping College Affordable: Government's Role in Promoting Educational Opportunity.* Washington, D.C.: Brookings Institution, 1991.

Merisotis, J. P. *Taxing Matters: College Aid, Tax Policy, and Equal Opportunity.* Boston: Education Resources Institute/Institute for Higher Education Policy, 1997.

Merisotis, J. P., and Parker, T. D. "College Debt and the New England Family." *Connection,* 1996, *11,* 18–19.

National Association of Student Financial Affairs Officers. *A Report to the Leaders of America's Colleges and Universities: Meeting the Challenge of Student Financial Aid.* Washington, D.C.: National Association of Student Financial Affairs Officers, 1995.

National Center for Education Statistics. *Enrollment, Fall 1995.* Washington, D.C.: Government Printing Office, 1997.

National Center for Education Statistics, *Postsecondary Financing Strategies: How Undergraduates Combine Work, Borrowing, and Attendance.* Washington, D.C.: Government Printing Office, 1998.

National Center for Education Statistics. *Annual Earning of Young Adults, by Educational Attainment.* Washington, D.C.: Office of Educational Research and Improvement, 1999.

Orfield, G. "Money, Equity, and College Access." *Harvard Education Review,* 1992, *62,* 337–372.

Pascarella, E. T., and Terenzini, P. T. *How College Affects Students: Findings and Insights from Twenty Years of Research.* San Francisco: Jossey-Bass, 1991.

Paulsen, M. B., and St. John, E. P. "The Financial Nexus Between College Choice and Persistence." In R. A. Voorhees (ed.), *Researching Student Aid: Creating an Action Agenda.* New Directions for Institutional Research, no. 95. San Francisco: Jossey-Bass, 1997.

Saxton, J., and Knight, S. *College Affordability: Tuition Tax Credits vs. Saving Incentives.* Washington, D.C.: Joint Economic Committee, 1997.

Scannell, J., and Simpson, K. *Shaping the College Experience Outside the Classroom.* Rochester, N.Y.: University of Rochester Press, 1996.

Stanton, M. "Cooperative Education: Working Toward Your Future." *Occupational Outlook Quarterly,* 1988, *32* (3), 22–29.

Stern, D. S., and Nakata, Y. F. "Paid Employment Among U.S. College Students: Trends, Effects, and Possible Causes." *Journal of Higher Education,* 1991, *62,* 25–43.

St. John, E. P. *Prices, Productivity, and Investment: Assessing Financial Strategies in Higher Education.* ASHE-ERIC Higher Education Report No. 3. Washington, D.C.: School of Education and Human Development, George Washington University, 1994.

Trach, J. S., and Harney, J. Y. "Impact of Cooperative Education on Career Development of Community College Students with and Without Disabilities." *Journal of Vocational Education Research,* 1998, *23,* 147–158.

U.S. Department of Commerce, Bureau of the Census. *School Enrollment: Social and Economic Characteristics.* Washington, D.C.: U.S. Government Printing Office, 1993.

U.S. Department of Commerce, Bureau of the Census. *More Education Means Higher Career Earning.* Washington, D.C.: U.S. Government Printing Office, 1994.

U.S. General Accounting Office. *Restructuring Student Aid Could Reduce Low-Income College Student Dropouts.* Washington, D.C.: U.S. Government Printing Office, 1995.

Van Gyn, G. "Investigating the Educational Benefits of Cooperative Education: A Longitudinal Study." *Journal of Cooperative Education,* 1997, *32,* 70–85.

ROBERT DEBARD is associate professor in the School of Leadership and Policy Studies at Bowling Green State University, where he specializes in budget management and finance in higher education. He was formerly dean and campus executive officer of Firelands College of Bowling Green State University.

5

Research indicates that student aid influences both first-time enrollment and persistence. This chapter describes how an understanding of the research can inform refinement in recruitment and retention strategies.

The Impact of Student Aid on Recruitment and Retention: What the Research Indicates

Edward P. St. John

Unfortunately, the research literature remains ambiguous regarding the impact of student financial aid on enrollment. Some researchers continue to hold doubts that student aid influences enrollment and persistence, while others continue to develop increasingly sophisticated methods in their analyses of aid-packaging strategies. This lingering controversy is potentially problematic for student affairs administrators who are concerned about ensuring that their colleges are affordable for current and potential students. This chapter examines the reasons for the controversy, then considers how research on college choice can inform recruitment strategies and how research on persistence can inform retention strategies.

The Complexities of Student Aid Research

Does aid make a difference? Though most professionals in higher education would say yes, that is not always the position taken by economists and other researchers who study the impact of student aid on enrollment. Consequently, policymakers do not always believe arguments that more aid is needed to increase freshman enrollment or to retain students. Consider the following comment from a study recently released by the U.S. Department of Education: "Again, either financial aid has no effect on PSE decisions, or the model's limitations, the entitlement nature of financial aid programs, and the combining of two very different data sets, are preventing *accurate predictions of financial aid received*" (Akerhielm, Berger, Hooker, and Wise, 1998, p. 64, emphasis added).

Policymakers reading these comments might look with skepticism on the arguments of aid administrators that more funding for student grants is needed, just as legislators may look skeptically on the claims by administrators of state grant programs that funding for state grants really is important. To untangle why this controversy lingers, it is necessary to consider a set of problems related to theory and methods. Both issues are examined briefly below.

The Theory Problem. Theory problems have contributed to conflicting interpretations of research on the impact of student aid. It is important for those involved in the policy discourse about student aid to understand some of the limitations of net-price theory (for example, Hansen, 1983) and the original student-institutional fit model (for example, Tinto, [1987] 1993). Below I briefly review some of the limitations of these theories. I choose these as examples because net-price theory is widely used by economists who evaluate student aid programs, and the institutional-fit model has had a substantial influence on emergence of enrollment management (Hossler, Bean, and Associates, 1990).

Net Price Reconsidered. The limitations of net-price theory dominate the policy dimension of the theory problem. In conceptualizing human capital theory, Becker (1964) speculates that (1) students consider the costs and benefits (both financial and personal) of attending college compared to those of not attending and (2) increasing subsidies to the families with financial need could reduce the costs and induce enrollment. The theory of net price evolved (Jackson and Weathersby, 1975; Leslie and Brinkman, 1988) essentially arguing that the enrollment rate would increase or decrease by a specified percentage (determined from a review of demand studies) for each $100 increment of net price (usually measured as tuition minus grants). However, when this concept of price response was used as a way of assessing the effects of federal student aid programs, most analysts concluded that changes in federal student aid did not make a difference (Hansen, 1983; Kane, 1995).

Research has confirmed that net-price theory oversimplified how students respond to prices and subsidies. Two decades ago, Dresch (1975) argued that students might respond differently to price subsidies than they do to prices, which would mean that the whole notion of a fixed response to net price was faulty. Subsequent studies have essentially confirmed many of Dresch's arguments (Des Jardins, Ahlburg, and McCall, 1999; St. John, 1990a, 1990b, 1994a; St. John and Starkey, 1995; Somers and St. John, 1997). When analysts take into account the full set of prices and subsidies facing students, enrollment patterns follow what we would expect from research on the effects of student aid on enrollment and persistence (St. John, 1994b; St. John and Elliott, 1994).

Hence student aid does make a difference in first-time and continuing enrollment decisions. The relationship between enrollment and the amount of money (Des Jardins, forthcoming) that colleges, states, and the federal government spend on grants is not as easy to predict as it was once thought. It is not as simple as applying a net-price ratio to a change in the amount of aid available (Kane, 1995). Rather, a more complex estimation procedure is needed to estimate how changes in tuition, grants, and loans influence different populations (St. John, 1993, 1994a; Trammel, 1995; Des Jardins, forthcoming). It is thus difficult for a public college president to communicate about complex simulation procedures to a legislative committee. Although it may be possible to predict the effects of changes in state financial aid policies (for example, Des Jardins, forthcoming), it is difficult to use and communicate about these estimates. It is equally difficult for a chief student aid officer to predict the net-tuition revenues from an increased allocation for grants. However, it may be increasingly necessary to make such calculations to defend institutional investments in grants.

What the Institutional-Fit Model Overlooked. The early institutional-fit persistence models did not give adequate treatment to the effects of student aid in persistence research (St. John, Cabrera, Nora, and Asker, forthcoming). Indeed, Vincent Tinto ([1987] 1993), the leading scholar in this arena, once argued that finances were a polite excuse for students dropping out of college. Similar logical arguments have even been made by economists, who have argued that if aid was adequate, students would not respond to aid amounts in their persistence (Manski, 1989). However, in the past decade especially, there have been substantial declines in government grants and there is growing evidence that student aid is no longer adequate to support persistence in many instances and that students respond to prices and subsidies in their persistence decisions (St. John, Cabrera, Nora, and Asker, forthcoming; St. John, Paulsen, and Starkey, 1996).

Further, there is also growing evidence that students may respond differently to tuition and subsidies in their persistence decisions than they do in their first-time enrollment decisions (St. John, Paulsen, and Starkey, 1996; St. John and Starkey, 1995). Student aid, along with college prices, makes a difference in persistence, as it does in first-time enrollment. However, it does not make the same difference. That is, a package that is sufficient to attract a student to a college may not be sufficient to keep her or him there once faced with the realities of the cost of living at the college of choice.

These complexities make it still more difficult to respond to policymakers' questions about student aid. However, the good news is that student aid does make a difference, even if it is not easy to untangle how and why it makes a difference. Before giving some practical guidance on how research on student aid can inform policy, it is necessary to consider a few methodological problems.

Methods Problems. Researchers interested in assessing the effects of student aid on first-time enrollment and persistence are confronted by complex methodological problems and data limitations. It is important for student services administrators to be aware of a couple of these limitations when they review student aid research and communicate with policymakers about research findings.

First, perceptions of college costs and the ability to pay have a direct influence on enrollment and persistence. Perceptions of costs are important for the recruitment process because colleges compete with each other for students, and many colleges are quite clever in the ways they construct tuition and aid policy. Indeed, perceptions of ability to pay and affordability have an influence on the college experience, as well as on eventual persistence decisions (Cabrera, Nora, and Castañeda, 1992, 1993; St. John, Paulsen, and Starkey, 1996). It is important for student affairs administrators to be aware of these complexities, which is why some of the recent research on ability to pay is noted below.

Second, to measure the direct effects of student aid, researchers need to control for family income (St. John, 1992; Somers, 1992). Income information is collected through the aid application process and can be used in workable models for research on the effects of aid (St. John, 1992; St. John, 1999; Somers and St. John, 1997). It is now possible for institutional researchers to assess routinely how an institution's aid-packaging strategy influences affordability in both first-time enrollment and persistence. Hence, although national and state studies can inform aid administrators about the context for institutional aid policy, locally developed studies are needed to let senior administrators know how their colleges are actually performing— whether their colleges remain affordable (for example, St. John, 1998).

Finally, there is now substantial research (Des Jardins, Ahlburg, and McCall, 1999; St. John and Starkey, 1995; St. John, Andrieu, Oescher, and Starkey, 1994; St. John, Paulsen, and Starkey, 1996; Somers and St. John, 1997) that can better inform interpretation of coefficients for aid variables derived from research on the effects of student aid. A negative and significant coefficient for an aid variable means that aid is insufficient, controlling for other factors that influence first-time enrollment and persistence. A positive coefficient means that receiving aid improves the probability of enrollment or persistence. And a neutral coefficient not only means that the variable is not significant, but that the receipt of aid essentially equalizes opportunity for enrollment or persistence, controlling for other variables in the model. Assuming the study cited above (that is, Akerhielm, Berger, Hooker, and Wise, 1998) was well designed, the neutral coefficient for aid means that at the particular point in time studied, student aid was adequate for the otherwise-average student to enroll.[1] However, there could have been inequities for some subpopulations, an issue that would require further analysis.

Making Sense of the Research. On the basis of these considerations, it is possible to reach some conclusions about the state of student aid research that can be informative for student affairs administrators, a topic addressed next. When appropriate logic and methods are used to assess the effects of student aid, it is possible to generate information that can inform policy decisions. I will consider first how the literature on the influence of student aid on college choice can inform recruitment strategies, then I will examine how research on the influence of aid on persistence can inform retention and budgeting processes. I hope this discussion provides a framework that helps facilitate better communications about the research as well.

The Impact of Student Aid on College Choice

There are some workable modeling approaches available for those who want to simulate the enrollment and budget effect of alternative aid strategies (Des Jardins, Ahlburg, and McCall, 1999; St. John, 1993, 1994a, 1999; Trammel, 1995). There are also some more practical ways that research on the effects of student aid can inform policy and practice. This section discusses four specific issues that merit consideration when attempting to use research on college choice to inform the recruitment process.

The Impact of Pricing Strategies. The simplest way to think about the impact of student aid in the recruitment and first-time enrollment processes is to consider its impact on individual cases. Frequently, admissions representatives are asked by parents whether they can renegotiate an aid offer. Some private colleges have gone so far as to give admissions staff some discretion over a certain level of changes they can make in the institutional portion of the aid package. However, this adaptive strategy can result in decreasing net-tuition revenues for increasing numbers of students. At the other extreme, there are many public colleges that have not made a sufficient investment in institutional grants, given the erosion in federal grants and tuition increases. Institutions that do not make sufficient investment in aid not only risk losing revenues from students who might otherwise enroll if tuition was lower or grant aid higher, but they can lose revenues due to reductions in persistence rates attributable to these conditions. These institutions also need to think about tuition and revenue linkages. There are three principles that should guide the use of aid to attract students to a campus (that is, to influence the college choice process).

First, *student aid makes a difference in affordability at virtually all types of institutions.* For several decades it was assumed that aid was consistently and positively associated with first-time enrollment (Jackson, 1978; Leslie and Brinkman, 1988; Manski and Wise, 1983; St. John, 1991). However, recent institutional studies indicate that student aid offers can have a negative association with first-time enrollment decisions by admitted applicants in both public and private colleges (Somers and St. John, 1997). This means that in the current context—with government-provided aid no longer being sufficient to promote continuous enrollment for students in the typical public four-year college—it is necessary for colleges to spend their own money on student grants. Hence, virtually all types of colleges and universities need to find additional revenues (from tuition, private gifts, and some other source) to optimize enrollment opportunity.[2]

Second, *it is important to establish a linkage between institutional budgeting and the aid-packaging strategies used in the recruitment process.* When institutions lose students they might be able to otherwise recruit, they lose revenues—from tuition and other sources (for example, tax subsidies in public colleges)—that they might otherwise be able to gain. However, when the aid costs are too high, they do not realize sufficient net revenue to afford to serve the students they attract. Therefore, institutions need to consider these linkages carefully each year in the budgeting process. When there is a problem, a range of options merits consideration, including reducing tuition and aid (Hamm, 1995; Rothman, 1995), along with continuation of the conventional approach to budgeting. The key is to optimize the impact of student aid on enrollment and revenues—taking the steps the institution can to keep the college affordable, while maintaining a fiscally responsible approach.

Third, *it is important to treat the relationship between institutional budgets and aid packaging as a dynamic process.* It is not a simple matter of making a one-time adjustment in aid and budgeting strategies to optimize aid packaging. Not only are competitors looking for competitive advantages, but federal policy on student aid seems continually in flux. It is also important to coordinate institutional strategies with government policies to the extent possible. This means that institutions need to be prepared to treat their aid budgets in flexible ways, making adjustments each year when the Pell award schedule is announced or when other external factors change in unexpected ways. Indeed, it is appropriate to treat the nexus between institutional budgeting and aid-packaging strategies as though it were an experimental process and to use an inquiry-based approach to make strategic adaptations (St. John, 1995).

The Impact of Government Grants. In the 1960s and 1970s, economists frequently argued for a high-tuition, high-aid approach to the funding of higher education (for example, Committee on Economic Development, 1973; Hansen and Weisbrod, 1967). In the 1970s, federal grants were increased to a level that approached this original conception, and there was some good empirical evidence that aid offers with grants were sufficient to promote access (Jackson, 1978; Manski and Wise, 1983; St. John and Noell, 1989). However, there is now growing evidence that government grants are no longer sufficient to promote access (Des Jardins, Ahlburg, and McCall, 1999; Heller, 1998; Somers and St. John, 1997). The decline in government grants in the past two decades, coupled with the steady increases in tuition, have created conditions under which government grants alone are inadequate for students who are loan averse.

Hence, both public and private colleges have reasons to consider investing in grants as a means of providing opportunity to students who are admitted. Some student aid researchers (for example, McPherson and Schapiro, 1998) recommend that the old standard of need-blind admissions and providing adequate grant aid be maintained. This is admirable. However, with the erosion in federal grants, this will probably be an increasingly difficult standard for many institutions to meet. Therefore, other forms of aid play an important role and deserve serious consideration when institutions develop their financial strategies.

The Impact of Loans, Work, and Tax Credits. The availability of other types of student aid also has an influence on student-enrollment decisions. It is abundantly apparent now that the new high-loan strategy of the federal government has had an influence on student first-time enrollment behavior (McPherson and Schapiro, 1998; Somers and St. John, 1997). Specifically, the curtailing of federal grants over the past two decades has influenced a larger percentage of low-income students to enroll in two-year colleges instead of four-year colleges (St. John, 1994b). There are several ways for institutional leaders to think about the strategic use of other forms of aid in the recruitment process.

First, there is evidence that middle-class students are especially responsive to loans in the initial-enrollment process (St. John, 1990a). Further, institutions that target self-help (loans and work study) have some potential advantages in recruitment. This approach has an appeal to upper-middle-income students who want to attend quality colleges, but the strategy has limited appeal to low-income applicants (Somers and St. John, 1997). One possible approach to increasing the appeal of loans and work to low-income students is to develop approaches that "forgive" portions of loans if students do not earn as much as is needed to repay in a timely way. Simulations suggest that such a process would actually be less costly than redirecting substantial portions of tuition revenue to grants (St. John, 1994a). The advantage of emphasizing other forms of aid is that it can keep prices lower than the now-conventional method of redirecting a portion of new tuition revenue to student grants.

Second, there is a new reason to rethink strategies for using alternative forms of aid as a recruitment tool. Institutions that have held down tuition and marketed themselves based on this principle have gained more students than might be otherwise predicted (Hamm, 1995; Rothman, 1995). By extension, institutions might have a competitive advantage if they strategically package aid and information in ways that indicate that self-help (loans, work, and tax credits) will be used as a means of constraining future price increases. This would create an expectation on the part of parents that annual tuition increases would be minimal. In addition, it could also build loyalty, if institutions carried through on these commitments.

Monitoring the Impact of Aid Offers. Colleges of all types need to develop systematic processes for reviewing their financial aid strategies. As long as government grants remain at levels that are insufficient to promote first-time enrollment and persistence in most four-year colleges, colleges will need to develop strategies for investing strategically in student aid. There are two probable consequences of not investing sufficiently in student aid: (1) a lower-than-expected yield of new students in the recruitment process and (2) a decline in persistence rates (an issue I consider further below). However, the consequences of investing too much in student aid include having too many students and too few resources to serve them. There is clearly a need to seek an optimum level of investment. There are three steps that institutions might want to consider.

First, institutions should routinely assess the effects of student aid offers. A new set of workable models for assessing the impact of student aid on enrollment has been proposed (St. John, 1992; Somers and St. John, 1997) and tested (Somers, 1992; Somers and St. John, 1997). These new models use admissions and student aid records and provide valid and reliable information on the effects of aid offers. These models can also be adapted for use in persistence studies (St. John, 1992; 1998; Somers, 1992). It is thus feasible for institutional researchers to provide information on the effects of student aid that can be used to inform institutional decisions about tuition and aid, as part of the annual budget process.

Second, institutions need a way of assessing the costs of their own investments in student aid. This can be done with simulations (Des Jardins, forthcoming; St. John, 1994a; Trammel, 1995) or through the systematic tracking of enrollment plans and budgets. Either way, institutions need systematically to assess the returns on their investments. These issues are most complex in institutions that attract large numbers of students with financial need. In these settings, constraining price increases, or even price reductions (Hamm, 1995; Rothman, 1995; St. John, 1995), may merit consideration.

Finally, it is important that institutions maintain an open experimental attitude about their investments in student aid. In the 1970s, some colleges began to invest more in student aid because their leaders thought this approach would give them a competitive advantage. However, in the past decade, more institutions have made these investments out of necessity. Given that more than two-thirds of students receive some type of aid in most public colleges and universities, there is a clear need to try out new approaches. When a large portion of students have financial need, it is difficult to realize substantial new net-tuition revenues from tuition increases (Trammel, 1995).

The Impact of Student Aid on Persistence

Increasingly, student aid is being recognized as a crucial factor in the persistence process. With the decline in the value of government grants, older notions that persistence decisions are independent of finances have given way to more systematic research on the impact of student aid. This section considers how research on the impact of student aid on persistence can inform retention practices.

The Critical Importance of Student Aid. A decade ago, many researchers doubted that student aid had an impact on persistence. Tinto (1975), the leading theorist on retention, once argued that financial problems were used as a polite excuse for dropping out, as was mentioned earlier in this chapter. However, Tinto ([1987] 1993) has reconceptualized his model based on a substantial body of new research on persistence. In fact, in some well-designed national studies, financial considerations explain more variance in the persistence process than variables related to the college experience and achievement in college (St. John, Paulsen, and Starkey, 1996). This does not mean that social and academic integration processes are not important—indeed, they are crucial, as well—however, students need to be able to afford to continue their enrollment. Three key findings about the effects of student aid are summarized below.

First, historically most studies found that student aid was positively associated with persistence. Prior to the 1990s, most research that examined the effects of student aid found there was a positive association between aid and persistence (for example, Astin, 1975; Leslie and Brinkman, 1988; St. John, 1990b; St. John, Kirshstein, and Noell, 1991; Terkla, 1985). Hence, the argument that finances were a polite excuse (for example, Tinto, [1987] 1993) for dropping out may have lacked grounding. However, as long as aid was adequate, it was at least possible that students could use finances as a "polite" excuse.

Second, in the 1990s, a growing number of researchers have discovered that student aid is no longer adequate to promote persistence (for example, St. John and Andrieu, 1995; St. John and Starkey, 1995; St. John, 1998; Des Jardins, Ahlburg, and McCall, 1999), especially in public colleges. Indeed, recent national studies have found that (1) grant aid was inadequate (or negatively associated with persistence) in public colleges and (2) grant aid was adequate (and neutral or positively associated with persistence) in private colleges (Paulsen and St. John, 1997; St. John, Oescher, and Andrieu, 1992). These differences are attributable to the amount private colleges invested from their own resources in grant aid. Public colleges did not make these adaptive changes, further reinforcing the notion that a supplemental institutional or state investment was needed to raise aid to an adequate level.

Third, students are aware of their financial constraints and consider these factors in both the college choice and persistence processes (St. John, Cabrera, Nora, and Asker, forthcoming). In fact, there is evidence that student perceptions of their ability to pay for college have an influence on their academic and social experiences in college (Cabrera, Nora, and Castañeda, 1992, 1993). Therefore, the inadequacy of student aid, relative to college prices, should be an issue of concern to college administrators because it can influence virtually all other aspects of college life.

Managing Debt Burden. Although loan default has become an important issue because of the threat of losing federal aid, the question of debt burden generally is not adequately addressed in the planning processes in institutions and at the state level. Recent studies have found that increasing debt burden has begun to take a toll on the opportunity to persist. One recent study of persistence in a private college found that debt had a negative influence on within-year persistence in 1993–1994, after average loan amounts increased, but not in prior years when loans were less central to aid packages (St. John, 1998). Further, a recent study of persistence by students enrolled at one large public university found that the negative effects of debt increased as students progressed through college. Loans were significant and positive for freshmen, but had a strong negative association with persistence for the same cohort of students when they were seniors (Des Jardins, Ahlburg, and McCall, 1999).

This means that the impact of turning to loans as an alternative to institutional grants needs to be closely monitored. As more institutions begin to experiment with alternative approaches to providing need-based subsidies to students, they will also need to monitor the effects of those strategies. At a minimum, institutions need to provide guidance to students on how to manage debt. Further, if the trend toward using loans as the primary source of aid continues, then more colleges and universities will be faced with difficult choices about their financial strategies.

The Nexus Between College Choice and Persistence. It is increasingly evident that there is a nexus between college choice and persistence: The perceptions students hold about affordability have a sustained influence on subsequent persistence decisions (St. John, Paulsen, and Starkey, 1996). Recent studies provide further evidence that there is great diversity in the ways students perceive college costs.

First, there are major differences in the perceptions of costs at public and private colleges (Paulsen and St. John, 1997). Students who choose private colleges because of high student aid are more likely to persist because aid is adequate. However, once the direct effects of student aid are controlled for in a well-designed analysis, then choosing a college because of aid can have a negative association with persistence. This means that students who are induced to choose a college because of a student aid offer can drop out because the college does not meet their expectations. Or if the college meets their expectations, they might not be able to afford continuous enrollment with the package they have been offered. In other words, inducing students to enroll because of aid offers may backfire. In contrast, in public colleges, students are choosing colleges because of low tuition and proximity to home and work. These students are much more concerned about managing college costs and paying for food and lodging.

Second, recent research indicates substantial social-class differences in the perceptions of college costs (Paulsen and St. John, 1999). Poor students were the most sensitive to prices and subsidies in the college-choice process. Working-class students (from lower-middle-income families) were more likely to consider work as important to manage their costs and debts to continue their enrollment. In contrast, middle-class (upper-middle-income) students faced tradeoffs about debt and living costs—borrowing to pay for housing and food—that influenced their eventual persistence decisions. Finally, upper-income students were more conscious of considering price in choosing a college and seemed to weigh these considerations carefully—the costs of attending versus the quality of education they receive—as they persisted through college.

Finally, another recent study found there were also differences in the ways perceptions of costs influenced persistence for students with different ethnic origins (Paulsen, St. John, and Carter, in preparation). African Americans valued student aid in their college choice and were more vulnerable to prices and living costs than other ethnic groups. Latino students were more likely to consider issues related to their ability to work and to avoid taking out loans during college. Further, persistence decisions by whites were also negatively influenced by debt and living costs.

Hence with escalating college costs, virtually all students are faced with a periodic need to reassess the value of their college choices as investment decisions. These periodic recalculations are not limited to students who have been thought to be financially at risk. Rather, with the growing use of debt, many more students are given cause to make these periodic assessments. When they do, they seem to consider their financial reasons for choosing a college in relation to the quality of their college experiences and the costs associated with continuing their enrollment.

The Implied Contract. The cumulative body of research on the impact of student aid on persistence indicates that there is an implied contract between institutions and students. The implied contract is formed in the recruitment process (forming initial expectations) and influences subsequent decisions about the commitment to continue enrollment. This process merits more explicit consideration in financial planning, as well as in the process of providing advice and support to students.

During the past two decades there have been substantial changes in federal student aid. Many private institutions have adjusted to these developments by allocating increasing portions of their tuition revenues to grant aid. Further, many private institutions are confronted by the need to make such adaptations because of erosion in public support. However, the consequences of these new strategies reach beyond the recruitment process to include persistence.

In particular, the older, often-used institutional strategy of modifying aid packages by reducing grants and adding loans for upper-division students merits review. One recent study found that putting more loans in at the end of the college experience had a negative effect on persistence by juniors and seniors (Des Jardins, Ahlburg, and McCall, 1999). There is also evidence that students reconsider their financial reasons for choosing their colleges when they make their subsequent decisions about persistence (Paulsen and St. John, 1997, 1999).

If institutional officials viewed the initial financial commitments made to students during the recruitment process as implied contracts, they would probably need to rethink these practices. One approach is to treat the initial aid award as a commitment that will be maintained through the four years of college. Another approach might involve including information to admitted students that indicates how their aid packages might change as they progress through college. This second approach is especially important in colleges that follow a practice of substituting loans for grants in the packages provided to upper-division students. In either case, it is important to communicate early and frequently with students about the institution's student aid packaging philosophy.

Conclusions

Not only does student aid make a difference in recruitment and retention, but it is also important that the linkages between these processes be carefully considered as an integral part of the annual budgeting process. While for a brief period in the 1960s and 1970s there was sufficient aid to promote equal opportunity, federal student aid is no longer adequate for this purpose. This means that colleges and universities need to plan carefully their investments in student aid.

Student aid offers have an immediate and direct effect on whether students enroll. They also have an influence on whether students can afford to continue their enrollment. In their initial college choices, students assess their possible college choices in relation to their personal situations. Some will consider proximity important, whereas others are more likely to value high aid or low tuition. Students also reconsider these financial reasons for attending as an integral part of their decisions to reenroll. Therefore, the effects aid has on persistence are inexorably linked to the effects it has on recruitment.

Further, it is increasingly evident that colleges must invest some of their own resources in grants to remain competitive. Without adequate student aid, growing numbers of students become periodic consumers, taking their courses as they can afford to do so. This means reductions in persistence rates, an outcome of increasing importance in the domain of public accountability. Institutions simply cannot afford to ignore these patterns.

By establishing a systematic process for assessing the effects of student aid on first-time enrollment and persistence, institutions can begin to manage their investments in student aid. Each year, as aid packages change due to federal, state, and institutional aid policies, students are faced with new choices about whether to enroll, where to attend, and whether to continue full time. By routinely assessing the effects of student aid on first-time enrollment and persistence, institutions can make better decisions about how much to invest in student grants, how much to emphasize loans and work, and whether to consider more drastic alternatives, such as price reductions.

Further, if more institutions were engaged in researching the effects of student aid, there would be a better empirical foundation for state and federal financial aid policy. It may be the responsibility of institutions to point out the inadequacy of support and the potential consequences of these inadequacies for economic development and tax-payer support of higher education.

Notes

1. One other possible problem with this study is that it has become more difficult to estimate the grant aid that nonapplicants would receive because of the large amount of discretionary institutional grants now being used. Therefore, models that use actual aid amounts awarded (St. John, 1992) are probably more reliable than models that rely on estimates of aid that might be awarded.

2. Unfortunately, in the current low-government-grant environment, institutions do need to be concerned about optimizing the use of their resources. Although I do not argue with the virtues of need-blind admissions (McPherson and Schapiro, 1998), I doubt whether most institutions can afford to fully fund need from their discretionary resources. Therefore, the next best alternative is to optimize the use of available funds.

References

Akerhielm, K., Berger, J., Hooker, M., and Wise, D. *Factors Related to College Enrollment: Final Report.* Princeton, N.J.: Mathtech, 1998.

Astin, A. W. *Preventing Students from Dropping Out.* San Francisco: Jossey-Bass, 1975.

Becker, G. S. *Human Capital: A Theoretical and Empirical Analysis with Special Reference to Education.* New York: National Bureau of Economic Research, 1964.

Cabrera, A. F., Nora, A., and Castañeda, M. B. "The Role of Finances in the Persistence Process: A Structural Model." *Research in Higher Education,* 1992, *33,* 571–593.

Cabrera, A. F., Nora, A., and Castañeda, M. B. "College Persistence: Structural Equations Modeling Test of an Integrated Model of Student Retention." *Journal of Higher Education,* 1993, *64,* 123–139.

Committee on Economic Development. *The Management and Financing of Colleges.* New York: Committee on Economic Development, 1973.

Des Jardins, S. L. "Simulating the Enrollment Effects of Changes in the Tuition Reciprocity Agreement Between Minnesota and Wisconsin." *Research in Higher Education,* forthcoming.

Des Jardins, S. L., Ahlburg, D. A., and McCall, B. P. "Simulating the Longitudinal Effects of Financial Aid on Student Departure from College." Unpublished manuscript, University of Iowa, 1999.

Dresch, S. P. "A Critique of Planning Models for Postsecondary Education: Current Feasibility, Potential Relevance, and a Prospectus for Future Research." *Journal of Higher Education,* 1975, *46,* 246–286.

Hamm, W. E. "The Walden College Tuition Reduction Experiment." In E. P. St. John (ed.), *Rethinking Tuition and Student Aid Strategies.* New Directions for Higher Education, no. 89. San Francisco: Jossey-Bass, 1995.

Hansen, W. L. "Impact of Student Aid on Access." In J. Froomkin (ed.), *The Crisis in Higher Education.* New York: Academy of Political Science, 1983.

Hansen, W. L., and Weisbrod, B. A. *Benefits, Costs, and Finance of Public Higher Education.* Chicago: Markham, 1967.

Heller, D. E. "A Comparison of the Tuition Price and Financial Aid Responsiveness of First-Time Students and Continuing College Students." Paper presented at the annual meeting of the Association for the Study of Higher Education, Miami, Fla., 1998.

Hossler, D., Bean, J., and Associates. *Strategic Management of College Enrollment.* San Francisco: Jossey-Bass, 1990.

Jackson, G. A. "Financial Aid and Student Enrollment." *Journal of Higher Education,* 1978, *49,* 548–574.

Jackson, G. A., and Weathersby, G. B. "Individual Demand for Higher Education." *Journal of Higher Education,* 1975, *46,* 623–652.

Kane, T. J. *Rising Public Tuition Levels and Access to College.* Cambridge, Mass.: National Bureau of Economic Research, 1995.

Leslie, L. L., and Brinkman, P. T. *The Economic Value of Higher Education.* Old Tappan, N.J.: Macmillan, 1988.

Manski, C. F. "Schooling as Experimentation: A Reappraisal of Postsecondary Dropout Phenomenon." *Economics of Education Review,* 1989, *8,* 305–312.

Manski, C. F., and Wise, D. A. *College Choice in America.* Cambridge, Mass.: Harvard University Press, 1983.

McPherson, M. S., and Schapiro, M. O. *The Student Aid Game: Meeting Need and Rewarding Talent in American Higher Education.* Princeton, N.J.: Princeton University Press, 1998.

Paulsen, M. B., and St. John, E. P. "The Financial Nexus Between College Choice and Persistence." *Researching Student Aid: Creating an Action Agenda.* New Directions for Institutional Research no. 95, San Francisco: Jossey-Bass, 1997.

Paulsen, M. B., and St. John, E. P. "Social Class and College Costs." Unpublished manuscript, 1999.

Paulsen, M. B., St. John, E. P., and Carter, D. F. "Ethnicity and Postsecondary Opportunity." Unpublished manuscript, 1999.

Rothman, M. L. "The Mills College Tuition Freeze Experience." In E. P. St. John (ed.), *Rethinking Tuition and Student Aid.* New Directions for Higher Education, no. 89. San Francisco: Jossey-Bass, 1995.

St. John, E. P. "Price Response in Enrollment Decisions: An Analysis of the High School and Beyond Sophomore Cohort." *Research in Higher Education,* 1990a, *31,* 161–176.

St. John, E. P. "Price Response in Persistence Decisions: An Analysis of the High School and Beyond Senior Cohort." *Research in Higher Education,* 1990b, *31,* 387–403.

St. John, E. P. "What Really Influences Minority Attendance? Sequential Analyses of the High School and Beyond Sophomore Cohort." *Research in Higher Education,* 1991, *32,* 141–158.

St. John, E. P. "Workable Models for Institutional Research on the Impact of Student Financial Aid." *Journal of Student Financial Aid,* 1992, 22 (3), 13–26.

St. John, E. P. "Untangling the Web: Using Price-Response Measures in Enrollment Projections." *Journal of Higher Education,* 1993, *63,* 165–187.

St. John, E. P. "Assessing Tuition and Student Aid Strategies: Using Price-Response Measures to Simulate Pricing Alternatives." *Research in Higher Education,* 1994a, *35,* 301–334.

St. John, E. P. *Prices, Productivity, and Investment: Assessing Financial Strategies in Higher Education.* ASHE-ERIC Higher Education Report No. 3. Washington, D.C.: George Washington University, 1994b.

St. John, E. P. "Rethinking Tuition and Student Aid Strategies." In E. P. St. John (ed.), *Rethinking Tuition and Student Aid Strategies.* New Directions for Higher Education, no. 89. San Francisco: Jossey-Bass, 1995.

St. John, E. P. "The Effects of Changes in Student Aid Policy on Persistence: A Case Study of a Private University." *Journal of Student Financial Aid,* 1998, *28* (1), 7–18.

St. John, E. P. "Evaluating State Grant Programs: A Case Study of Washington's Grant Program." *Research in Higher Education,* 1999, *40,* 149–170.

St. John, E. P., and Andrieu, S. C. "The Influence of Price Subsidies on Within-Year Persistence by Graduate Students." *Higher Education,* 1995, *29,* 143–168.

St. John, E. P., Andrieu, S. C., Oescher, J., and Starkey, J. B. "The Influence of Student Aid on Persistence by Traditional College-Age Students in Four-Year Colleges." *Research in Higher Education,* 1994, *35,* 455–480.

St. John, E. P., Cabrera, A. F., Nora, A., and Asker, E. H. "Economic Influences on Persistence." In J. M. Braxton (ed.), *Rethinking the Departure Puzzle: New Theory and Research.* Nashville, Tenn.: Vanderbilt University Press, forthcoming.

St. John, E. P., and Elliott, R. J. "Reframing Policy Research: A Critical Examination of Research on Federal Aid Programs." In J. C. Smart (ed.) *Higher Education: Handbook of Theory and Practice.* Vol. 10. New York: Agathon, 1994.

St. John, E. P., Kirshstein, R., and Noell, J. "The Effects of Student Aid on Persistence: A Sequential Analysis of the High School and Beyond Senior Cohort." *Review of Higher Education,* 1991, *14,* 383–406.

St. John, E. P., and Noell, J. "The Effects of Student Financial Aid on Access to Higher Education: An Analysis of Progress with Special Consideration of Minority Enrollment." *Research in Higher Education,* 1989, *30,* 563–581.

St. John, E. P., Oescher, J., and Andrieu, S. C. "The Influence of Prices on Within-Year Persistence by Traditional College-Age Students in Four-Year Colleges." *Journal of Student Financial Aid,* 1992, 22 (2), 27–38.

St. John, E. P., Paulsen, M. B., and Starkey, J. B. "The Nexus Between College Choice and Persistence." *Research in Higher Education,* 1996, *37,* 175–220.

St. John, E. P., and Starkey, J. B. "An Alternative to Net Price: Assessing the Influence of Prices and Subsidies on Within-Year Persistence." *Journal of Higher Education,* 1995, *66,* 156–186.

Somers, P. *A Dynamic Analysis of Student Matriculation Decisions in Urban Public Universities.* Unpublished doctoral dissertation, University of New Orleans, 1992.

Somers, P., and St. John, E. P. "Interpreting Price Response in Enrollment Decisions: A Comparative Institutional Study." *Journal of Student Financial Aid,* 1997, *29* (3), 15–36.

Terkla, D. G. "Does Financial Aid Enhance Undergraduate Persistence." *Journal of Student Financial Aid,* 1985, *15* (3), 11–18.

Tinto, V. "Dropout from Higher Education: A Theoretical Synthesis of Recent Research." *Review of Educational Research,* 1975, *45,* 89–125.

Tinto, V. *Leaving College: Rethinking the Causes and Cures of Student Attrition.* (2nd ed.) Chicago: University of Chicago Press, 1993. (Originally published 1987.)

Trammel, M. L. "Estimating the Enrollment Effects of a Midyear Surcharge." In E. P. St. John (ed.), *Rethinking Tuition and Student Aid Strategies.* New Directions in Higher Education, no. 89. San Francisco: Jossey-Bass, 1995.

EDWARD P. ST. JOHN is professor and chair of the higher education program at Indiana University, where he is also director of the Indiana Education Policy Center.

6

The strategic use of campus-based financial aid has become an integral part of enrollment management strategies. This chapter examines how colleges and universities are using financial aid to achieve enrollment and financial objectives.

The Role of Financial Aid in Enrollment Management

Don Hossler

The concept of enrollment management emerged in the late 1970s and early 1980s. In 1976, Jack Maguire, a faculty member in physics who was drafted into an administrative position, started to use the term *enrollment management* to describe a synergistic approach to influencing college enrollments he was putting into place at Boston College. In the early 1980s, Kruetner and Godfrey published an article about their enrollment management efforts at Long Beach State University. Soon afterwards, a number of articles, monographs, and books began to emerge on the topic of enrollment management (see for example Baldridge, Kemerer, and Green, 1982; Hossler, 1984; Muston, 1985).

Most of these early approaches to enrollment management included the office of financial aid, and acknowledged the role that pricing and financial aid played in influencing student enrollment decisions. Nevertheless, compared with the landscape of today, these early efforts to link financial aid within the broader concept of enrollment management seem simplistic. The role of financial aid within enrollment management has come a long way in just fifteen to twenty years.

However, in order to discuss the more sophisticated and complex role of financial aid in enrollment management, it is first necessary to provide an introduction to the concept of enrollment management. Within the context of an enrollment management framework, I will explore the role of financial aid on new student recruitment and retention. I will also examine the ethical issues related to the use of campus-based aid to achieve enrollment management objectives.

Understanding Enrollment Management

On most campuses there are multiple purposes for creating and sustaining enrollment management organizations. However, the purposes always focus on attracting and retaining students. These goals typically include efforts to increase the number of new students, plans to diversify the student body, efforts to retain more students, and a desire to enroll more high-ability students or students with special talents (athletics, music, theater, and so on). Administrators and faculty often assume that the only goal of enrollment management is to increase the number of new students. Senior leadership on many college campuses is equally interested in enrolling more nonresident students, more students of color, more high-ability students, or all such groups. These, too, can become important goals for enrollment managers.

A number of definitions of enrollment management have been offered by practitioners and scholars (see for example Hossler and Bean, 1990; Baldridge, Kemerer, and Green, 1982; Muston, 1985). These definitions share many common elements. Hossler and Bean (1990) define enrollment management as "an organizational concept and a systematic set of activities designed to enable educational institutions to exert more influence over their student enrollments. Organized by strategic planning and supported by institutional research, enrollment management activities concern student college choice, transition to college, student attrition and retention, and student outcomes. These processes are studied to guide institutional practices in the areas of new student recruitment and financial aid, student support services, curriculum development, and other academic areas that affect enrollments, student persistence, and student outcomes from college" (p. 5).

As a concept, enrollment management is broad in scope. Hossler and Bean (1990, pp. 5–6) suggest that "the key elements of enrollment management" are (1) using institutional research to position the campus in the marketplace, examine the correlates to student persistence, and develop appropriate marketing and pricing strategies; (2) monitoring student interests and academic program demand; (3) matching student demand with curricular offerings that are consistent with institutional mission; and (4) paying attention to academic, social, and institutional factors that affect student retention.

However, enrollment management is not only an organizational strategy to achieve enrollment goals, it can also be a tool to achieve other important goals. Because campus-based financial aid has become such an important part of enrollment management strategies, enrollment management efforts have also become an integral part of campus financial and budgeting strategies. The effects of new student enrollments and campus-based aid programs on net tuition revenue have a pronounced effect on the economic health and vitality of colleges and universities. Hence, enrollment management is not only part of an enrollment strategy, it has also become a budgeting strategy.

Enrollment management should also be viewed as a key part of an institutional positioning strategy. In the eyes of many external stakeholders, as well as prospective students, the size of the enrolled student body, the selectivity indicators of enrolled students (for example, average class rank or SAT score for an entering class, or *U.S. News and World Report* rankings), and the demographic characteristics of the students who enroll play a major role in defining colleges and universities. Along with location, cost, academic program offerings, and the extent to which a campus emphasizes research or teaching, the characteristics of the enrolled students create the market position of a campus in the eyes of external audiences. Therefore, enrollment management goals must be carefully linked to institutional positioning goals.

Although *enrollment management* has a broad and encompassing definition, on many campuses this term has been used to describe only activities focusing on the areas of recruitment and student financial aid. Clearly these are key aspects of enrollment management, but a comprehensive approach goes far beyond these two areas alone. Student academic success and student persistence are also important to successful enrollment management. In addition, enrollment management is a data-driven, analytical enterprise. Strategic decisions about pricing and institutional positioning, as well as tactical decisions about marketing activities and financial aid packages, can be improved through the use of sound research and evaluation.

As I have already noted, early enrollment management models were based on simplistic assumptions of the impact of financial aid and pricing strategies. In more recent years, enrollment management organizations and offices of budgeting and finance on college campuses are using sophisticated multivariate analyses to help them craft tuition policies and financial aid programs that will help campuses achieve their enrollment and budget goals. In ten years, financial aid has moved from being one of many components of enrollment management efforts to being one of the key factors.

Purposes of Financial Aid

Before examining the current role of financial aid in enrollment management, it is useful to review briefly the purposes of financial aid. Some financial aid administrators and scholars of financial aid policy have been critical of the growing use of financial aid to achieve enrollment goals. To address these concerns later in this chapter, I will quickly review the traditional purposes of financial aid. Many critics of current campus-based aid strategies that focus on the effects of aid on influencing student enrollment decisions focus exclusively on the original goals of federal financial aid programs that were designed in the 1960s and 1970s. These federal programs, and many of the state programs that were created as a result of the State Student Incentive Grant Program, focused on increasing student access to higher education among low- and moderate-income families. Clearly, these are important and laudable goals. However, the purpose of federal, state, and institutional financial aid programs has always been broader and more complex than access and equity, including rewarding past service to the nation, stimulating more students majoring in areas where there are labor shortages, remedying past injustices, and enhancing the stability of colleges and universities (McPherson and Schapiro, 1991).

It is evident that the purposes and goals of financial aid have always been complex and diverse. The noted historian of higher education, Frederick Rudolph (1990), when describing the events of the nineteenth century, and Michael McPherson, a distinguished economist who specializes in the economics of higher education, both conclude that helping maintain the fiscal health of colleges and universities has always been one of the purposes of campus-based financial aid programs.

The Role of Financial Aid in Influencing College Enrollment Decisions and Student Retention

It is difficult to understand why financial aid has become such an important part of enrollment management efforts without summarizing the research on the impact of financial aid on prospective college students and enrolled college students.

Financial Aid and Enrollment Decisions. Research on this area has increased dramatically in recent years. The higher education system in the United States is diverse, and it is not possible in this chapter to provide a detailed discussion of how campus-based financial aid policies affect students considering individual institutions. How students considering a regional private comprehensive college might respond to campus-based financial aid programs would be quite different from how students applying to a public doctoral-granting flagship university would respond. Students who plan to live at home and attend a commuter campus have price thresholds different from students considering rural residential institutions. In addition, institutional characteristics such as selectivity, reputation, and depth of applicant pool also influence how prospective students are influenced by campus-based financial aid programs. For example, an Ivy League college with a very deep applicant pool does not necessarily have to offer as much financial aid to induce students to enroll as a regional, less well known private college with a smaller applicant pool might have to offer.

It is also difficult to separate the impact of tuition on student enrollments from the effects of student financial aid. Tuition cost is clearly a signaling device for students and parents. The problem is that effects of tuition costs and financial aid do not uniformly affect the decisions of prospective or currently enrolled college students. Some students and families automatically equate higher cost with higher quality. Other potential college matriculants automatically exclude higher cost institutions because they believe they cannot afford them. They often do this without any knowledge of possible financial aid awards. The difficult task for most institutions is to try to determine how *most* of the students and families in their markets react to price. The word *most* is emphasized here because reactions will not be uniform among all potential students. Because of the interaction effects between tuition costs and financial aid programs it is possible for enrollment managers, in consultation with other senior campus administrators, to simulate several approaches to tuition costs and financial aid. Some private and public colleges maintain low costs and offer very little institutional financial aid. These institutions rely on low costs as the primary financial factor in helping achieve enrollment goals. Other private and public institutions[1] pursue a high-tuition, high-aid strategy. Often referred to as the "Robin Hood" strategy, these institutions set higher tuition rates and then target campus-based scholarship programs toward students whom they seek to enroll. The scholarships lower the net cost of attendance and influence the matriculation decisions of students who receive these offers. In this section, the focus is on the effects of campus-based financial aid on student enrollment decisions. However, it is important to keep in mind that some colleges and universities use low tuition costs rather than financial aid to help manage their enrollments.

To examine the complex effects of financial aid on the college enrollment decisions of traditional age students, it is helpful to draw from two strands of research. These include meta-analyses of the effects of financial aid on student enrollment decisions and research on the college choice process.

Several reviews and meta-analyses of the effects of financial aid on enrollment decisions are available (Heller, 1997; Jackson, 1978; Leslie and Brinkman, 1987; St. John, 1990). Each of these reaches similar conclusions. One key finding is that receiving a financial aid award has a significant positive effect on the likelihood that a student will enter the institution that has made the financial aid offer. Indeed, these reviews conclude that the effect of just receiving an award, regardless of the amount, equals or exceeds the effects of the amount of the award. This conclusion is not meant to infer that the amount of a campus-based award does not influence college matriculation decisions. The amount of an aid offer does matter. Several studies have demonstrated that enrollment decisions are influenced by the amount of financial aid awards (Chapman and Jackson, 1987; Tierney, 1980). For emphasis, however, it should be noted that the effects of aid interact in complex ways. Students may turn down a generous financial aid package from a small regional private college if they are admitted to a prestigious Ivy League college that offers no financial aid. Furthermore, research has consistently found that African American students and Latino students are more cost sensitive and more responsive to financial aid offers than majority students of similar socioeconomic background (Hossler, Braxton, and Coopersmith, 1989; Paulsen, 1990). Similarly, it typically requires larger scholarships to influence the enrollment decisions of high-ability students. These students are heavily recruited by many colleges and universities and are often offered many large scholarships. These students are also more likely to be interested in institutions with higher levels of prestige and greater selectivity. For these reasons, many colleges and universities need to offer higher-ability students larger scholarship awards if they wish to influence their enrollment decision on the basis of financial aid offers (Chapman and Jackson, 1987).

One limitation of this line of research is that many of the studies on which these conclusions are based were conducted before non-need-based campus aid had become as common as it is now. Growing competition for college students of all ability levels, but especially the competition for high-ability students, has resulted in greater amounts of campus general fund money being invested in scholarships designed to influence the enrollment decisions of students. Hence, it is possible that students have become even more responsive to the amount of their financial aid awards. Nevertheless, the cumulative results of these studies indicate that colleges and universities should continue to emphasize that campus-based aid, even modest awards, may have a positive impact on the matriculation decisions of prospective students. These findings lead to two important conclusions about the effect of financial aid on student enrollment decisions. First, and not surprisingly, the amount of financial aid students are offered has an effect on the decisions they make as to which college or university to attend. Second, financial aid offers also have psychological benefits for prospective students.

In a recent book, *Going to College: How Social, Financial, Educational Experiences Influence the Decisions Students Make* (Hossler, Schmit, and Vesper, 1998), the effects of how perceived costs, financial aid, and other factors influence the college enrollment decisions of high school students as they move from the ninth grade through high school graduation were carefully researched. The authors found that one of the primary factors that parents, and later students, consider when dropping and adding colleges to the list of schools they are considering is the perceived costs and the probabilities of receiving financial aid. This process of dropping and adding schools starts as early as the tenth grade. Furthermore, parents play a key role in this process. Simple statements such as "We can't afford to send you to that school" or "You can attend that school if you get a scholarship" can have a powerful impact on which institutions students seriously consider. These findings are consistent with Jackson's meta-analysis of the effects of financial aid on student enrollment decisions. Jackson (1978) concluded that many students fail to consider or needlessly eliminate colleges and universities that might have been good choices for them because they believe they cannot afford to attend these schools. These findings lead to two additional conclusions. Total cost of attendance influences the decisions of students long before they get to the point of selecting which college to attend. As a result, the timing of when students (and their parents) learn about actual or possible financial aid packages can influence the planning for going to college, even at very early stages of the process.

In sum, these findings indicate that colleges and universities can use campus-based financial aid to help them achieve their enrollment goals. Financial aid awards, along with tuition costs, may exert a strong influence on the number and types of prospective students that consider attending individual colleges and universities.

The most widely discussed campus-based response to the effects of financial aid on the college decisions of students in the context of the current financial pressures placed on institutions, students, and families is some variant of the Robin Hood strategy. This approach raises tuition and uses large portions of the increase to provide financial aid to prospective college students in order to induce them to matriculate. Although these financial aid inducements might be used to meet student financial need, the intent behind the strategy is to use the award as a merit award that will help individual campuses more effectively "court" or recruit students with higher grades, with more talent, or with lower levels of financial need. In the admissions and financial aid community there is a great deal of discussion of financial aid leveraging. Aid leveraging is an analytical tool that enables admissions and financial aid administrators to estimate the amount of financial aid (regardless of formal need formulas) that would be necessary to increase the probability that a student with a specified set of characteristics would enroll. These characteristics often include variables such as academic performance, socioeconomic status, major, ethnicity, place of residence, and special talents. It must be remembered, however, that this approach is not without increased costs. Institutions have to increase their tuition, increase the education and general (E&G) portion of the budget that is allocated to financial aid, or both.

The increased focus on ratios between tuition income and financial aid expenditures has changed the discussion on many campuses. In the early 1970s, even among private institutions, it was uncommon to have more than 10 to 15 percent of total tuition revenue returned in the form of scholarships or discounts to students (Hossler, 1984). Currently, it is not uncommon for private institutions to have discount rates as high as 25 to 30 percent. Institutional policymakers often become more concerned about net tuition revenue than total student enrollment. Originally, Robin Hood strategies were used by private sector institutions. Nevertheless, public institutions have also started to use this technique to optimize revenues.

Public flagship institutions, however, face difficult problems with this approach for their out-of-state student markets. If they continue to raise their tuition, they run the risk of reaching tuition levels that come close to the costs of more selective private institutions. Most of these private colleges and universities award significant amounts of student financial aid. These large scholarships and increased competition for high-ability students make it increasingly difficult for public flagships to recruit out-of-state students without investing even more in their financial aid programs.

It is unlikely that tuition leveraging can continue indefinitely. The costs of competing over the size of tuition discounts will eventually cause cost increases that go beyond what students are willing to pay (Edgerton, 1993). In addition, as the amount allocated to financial aid awards increases, institutional investments in the academic infrastructure and campus facilities decrease. Eventually, campus administrators will be forced to make difficult decisions and to evaluate whether or not institutional resources would be better invested in other areas. In addition, the ever present threat of enforced cost containment in the public sector and the competitive pressures in the private sector will act to constrain the use of high-tuition, high-aid strategies.

Not all colleges and universities, however, are pursuing high-tuition, high-aid approaches. Some regional public and private institutions have sustained enrollments by keeping costs low. They have a sound reputation in local markets and use their cost advantages as the principal mechanism for attracting students. Institutions that attract primarily commuting students (for example, community colleges and metropolitan institutions) are also hesitant to raise their costs too high. A large proportion of their enrollments are part-time students who are very cost sensitive and may not take enough classes to qualify for most forms of financial aid.

Financial Aid and Student Retention. Financial aid can also have an impact on the retention of currently enrolled students. In Chapter Five, Edward St. John discusses the relationships between financial aid and student persistence in detail. For this reason, the impact of financial aid on student persistence will not be examined in depth here. Enrollment management practitioners, however, should keep in mind that how financial aid influences student retention is more complex than how it affects student enrollment decisions. Because federal, state, and institutional financial aid policies change so frequently, it is impossible for enrollment managers to make definitive statements about the effects of financial aid on matriculation and retention. Analyses of the effects of aid on student matriculation and persistence decisions have to be replicated annually in order for enrollment managers to be confident that campus policies are having the optimal desirable effect on student enrollments. In addition, readers should keep in mind that variables drawn for sociological models of student departure such as the Tinto model (1987) or the Bean model (1980) find that effects of financial aid are smaller than factors such as academic and social integration or academic success. Therefore, these factors are likely to be more promising areas for intervention for most enrollment managers seeking to improve student persistence.

Using Financial Aid to Achieve Institutional Goals

The use of econometric techniques to determine the effects of financial aid on student enrollments and increased use of tuition leveraging approaches have changed how financial aid and tuition policies are determined. Organizational linkages of offices of admissions, financial aid, and academic units through enrollment management structures have resulted in the strategic use of financial aid throughout the recruitment and retention process. To reinforce the use of financial aid to achieve institutional goals, it is helpful to provide an overview of the annual process of developing institutional financial aid policies and examine how enrollment managers may use these policies in an optimal fashion to realize enrollment and revenue goals.

The Goal-Setting Process. For decades, discussions about tuition rates, campus-based financial aid policies, and enrollment targets were based on efforts to anticipate what other competing institutions were going to do, and were combined with the efforts of senior campus policymakers to balance the budget. Often goals for the number of newly enrolled students for the coming year were set solely on the basis of past trends and revenue goals for the campus. However, these new analytical techniques now permit simulations of the financial aid costs of achieving desired enrollment goals and the overall impact on the total campus budget. The steps and the timing of the process may vary from campus to campus; however, the basic framework is likely to be similar for all institutions.

Phase One. The offices of admissions and financial aid generate data sets that include as much information as possible about the demographic and financial characteristics of the entire student applicant pool, contacts with the admissions and financial aid offices prior to matriculation or nonmatriculation, and any campus financial aid offers that were made to matriculants and nonmatriculants. The data file is typically given to the office of institutional research or an external consultant in situations where campuses are not staffed to conduct such analyses. This process usually begins in the late summer or immediately after the school year begins. This is always conducted at this time of the year to allow for comparisons to be made between students in the file who were admitted and did not enroll and those who did enroll. It is possible to begin the analysis by using students who have paid deposits rather than using enrolled students if most students who pay enrollment deposits subsequently enroll. It is more desirable, however, to generate the analysis after the semester begins so that actual matriculants can be compared with those who did not enroll.

Phase Two. The office of institutional research (or consultants) works closely with enrollment managers during the process of data analysis. Anomalies in the results are frequently found. Those doing the analysis often lack sufficient knowledge of the activities of the offices of admissions and financial aid or the policies of competitor institutions. As a result, some results may be misinterpreted. The first round of analysis seldom answers all the questions about the effects of financial aid on total new student enrollment, student diversity, high-ability students, and so forth. For this reason, the analysis phase is an iterative process. Analysis leads to additional questions, which in turn lead to additional analysis until representatives of the enrollment management office have identified two to three sets of optimal approaches to achieving enrollment and revenue goals.

Phase Three. These scenarios are next considered by the offices of financial aid and admissions. This is to ensure that these two offices can implement the proposed financial aid policies. Sometimes the analyses can lead to proposals that would be very difficult for a financial aid office to administer. For example, large public universities rely heavily on computer software to manage the awarding of financial aid. If a proposed policy requires large numbers of manual interventions into the process it may not be possible to implement some aspects of a policy, or at least the financial aid office may require additional personnel.

Phase Four. It is rare for even vice-presidents for enrollment management to be authorized to set final policies about financial aid because of their substantial impact on total campus revenues. Usually, the senior enrollment manager will next present two or three campus-based financial aid plans to the president and other senior members of the president's cabinet. In large institutions, academic deans may also be part of the enrollment management and financial aid decision-making process. Indeed, at some large institutions, this entire process is completed to derive different financial aid programs for each academic school such as a college of arts and science or a college of engineering. This advisory process leads to a final decision about the scope and purpose of campus-based financial aid for the coming year.

Executing the Plan. Once the parameters of the financial aid plan are determined, it is up to the enrollment management division to implement the plan. One of the tensions in the process outlined above is the desire of the enrollment management staff to inform prospective students as soon as possible about any financial aid they might potentially receive. The degree of concern about early information about financial aid varies according to the depth or quality of an institution's applicant pool. There is such high demand for admissions to highly selective institutions that these colleges and universities can wait until very late in the enrollment decision process to inform students of their actual aid packages. Colleges and universities with modest levels of selectivity and shallow applicant pools have a greater need to get information about possible financial aid awards to prospective students as early as possible in order to increase the likelihood that they will continue to keep them on the list of schools that students are seriously considering.

Financial aid award letters, however, should not be limited only to communicating the amount of financial aid. Many campus scholarships are also linked with selection for special academic programs, student leadership programs, or other special talents (music, athletics, and so on). Recruitment letters, congratulatory phone calls, or special on-campus events for those selected should emphasize the importance of being selected as well as the financial aid award. Linking recruitment and financial aid activities is likely to result in making a greater positive impression on an admitted student than would either the scholarship or being selected for the special academic or leadership program alone.

Finally, it is also important to analyze the effects of the financial aid strategy continuously. If anticipated yield rates appear to be falling behind projections during the course of the year, it is possible to revise the plan or develop additional recruitment strategies that can be used in conjunction with financial aid awards.

Ethical Concerns

The rise of campus-based merit aid and tuition leveraging strategies to achieve enrollment and revenue has been criticized within the higher education community (Edgerton, 1993; McPherson and Schapiro, 1991). Critics argue that campus-based aid should be used to assure access and equity for all students. They note that tuition discounting and financial aid leveraging strategies are also leading to higher tuition rates so that colleges and universities can use the additional revenue to fund merit scholarships for students who might otherwise qualify for additional need-based financial aid in order to be able to afford to attend a college or university of their choice. These assertions are correct. No current observer of financial aid policy would disagree with these observations. However, these criticisms have to be placed in context.

First, as already noted, the emergence of a national effort to use financial aid to enhance equity and access only appeared in the 1960s. For most of the history of higher education, institutional financial aid was focused on institutional priorities or was directed by the wishes of individuals who endowed scholarships. Critics often sound as though the current focus of campus-based aid on enrollment and revenue goals is a reversion of long-standing campus policies. More important, throughout the 1970s and 1980s, except for a small number of elite and well-endowed institutions, most colleges and universities relied on federal and state governments to meet financial need. Few campuses, especially public universities, provided large amounts of need-based aid out of campus general fund revenues. This is not to suggest that the use of a need-based focus for all forms of financial aid should not be a goal for federal, state, and institutional policymakers. However, few colleges and universities are able to achieve this ideal, and those that do are typically wealthy institutions with deep applicant pools.

This leads to the next observation about the use of campus financial aid to achieve enrollment management goals. For the past twenty-five years, most colleges and universities competed aggressively for students to achieve their financial and educational goals. Predictive modeling and tuition leveraging became an important part of the competitive environment. Schools that do not engage in these practices are often placed at a competitive disadvantage. In their recent book, *The Student Aid Game*

(1998), McPherson and Schapiro describe the difficult circumstances many colleges find themselves in as they attempt to equalize concerns for equity, efficiency, financial responsibility, and balance institutional budgets. Sandy Baum (1998), an economist who specializes in federal financial aid policy, concludes, "Balancing long-term and short-term goals, considering the interplay between the ability to pay and willingness to pay, thinking of financial aid as part of a pricing policy, and understanding the mutually reinforcing aspects of equity and efficiency all lead to the suggestion that the goals of both equity and strategic planning must enter into financial aid allocation decisions" (p. 16).

In the past, it was common for presidents and academic administrators to set targets for increasing the number of total new students or the number of students of color with little sense of the resources required to achieve these goals. Predictive modeling for financial aid is an important tool in helping institutions prioritize their goals. The use of analytical techniques such as predictive modeling helps campus administrators understand the potential cost of investing in financial aid or other approaches to strengthen recruitment or retention efforts. For example, academic support programs are effective tools enabling more disadvantaged students to be successful and persist. Predictive modeling enables comparisons of the costs and benefits of investing more funds in financial aid or academic support programs. When a board of trustees, or a college president, announces a plan to increase the number of Latino students, multivariate analysis enables campus administrators to identify the costs that will be required to fund such an initiative. Critics of the use of predictive modeling fail to take into account how it can be used to make a case for more need-based aid as well as merit aid on campuses.

More vexing problems related to the use of campus-based financial aid scholarships to influence student enrollment include the conditions of scholarships. Some campuses only guarantee scholarships for one year. Other colleges and universities establish grade-point-average renewal criteria so high that many returning students who were counting on the scholarship to help finance their college education may not see their aid renewed in succeeding years. These tactics raise obvious ethical questions.

The Future

The next fifteen years will be an interesting period for enrollment managers and the use of financial aid in recruitment and retention. Many private colleges and universities are struggling to reduce the amount of general fund revenue spent on scholarships, thus lowering their discount rates. Conversely, there has been an increase in the use of campus-based financial aid to meet enrollment goals at public institutions. However, the use of tuition discounting at public institutions has been limited primarily to attract more nonresident students. Nonresidents are attractive because of the higher tuition rates they pay.

The "baby boomlet" is upon us and as a result, colleges and universities may not have to rely as much on financial aid to achieve enrollment objectives. There will continue to be high levels of competition for high-ability students, students of color, and students with special talents. What we may see is a decrease in merit aid offers to strong, but not excellent students. Currently, it is not unusual for students in the top 20 to 25 percent of their class with SAT scores of approximately 1200 to receive generous campus scholarships. These students may see a decline in financial aid offers as the number of graduating high school students increases.

It is important to keep in mind, however, that increases in the size of the high school cohorts are not consistent in all regions of the United States. Schools with shallow, regional, applicant pools located in areas that are projecting modest increases in high school graduates will continue to use campus-based financial aid to help them achieve their enrollment goals, institutional positioning goals, and financial objectives.

Note

1. Among public institutions, the high-tuition, high-aid strategy is most often used for nonresident students. Public institutions typically charge higher tuition rates for nonresident students, and some public colleges and universities then return partial discounts in the form of campus scholarships.

References

Baldridge, J. V., Kemerer, F. R., and Green, K. C. *Enrollment Management in the Eighties: Factors, Actors, and Impact.* Washington, D.C.: American Association for Higher Education, 1982.

Baum, S. "Balancing Act: Can Colleges Achieve Equal Access and Survive in a Competitive Market?" *College Board Review,* 1998, *186,* 12–17.

Bean, J. P. "Dropouts and Turnover: The Synthesis of a Causal Model of Student Attrition." *Research in Higher Education,* 1980, *12,* 155–187.

Chapman, R. C., and Jackson, R. *College Choices of Academically Able Students: The Influence of No-Need Financial Aid and Other Factors.* Research Monograph No. 10. New York: College Board, 1987.

Edgerton, R. "The Public Scrutiny of the Value of Higher Education." *AAHE Bulletin,* 1993, *45* (10), 3–7.

Heller, D. "Student Price Response in Higher Education: An Update to Leslie and Brinkman." *Journal of Higher Education,* 1997, *56,* 735–750.

Hossler, D. *Enrollment Management: An Integrated Approach.* New York: College Board, 1984.

Hossler, D., and Bean, J. P. *The Strategic Management of College Enrollments.* San Francisco: Jossey-Bass, 1990.

Hossler, D., Braxton, J., and Coopersmith, G. "Understanding Student College Choice." In J. Smart (ed.), *Higher Education: Handbook of Theory and Research.* Vol. 4. New York: Agathon, 1989.

Hossler, D., Schmit, J., and Vesper, N. *Going to College: How Social, Economic, and Educational Factors Influence the Decisions Students Make.* Baltimore: Johns Hopkins University Press, 1998.

Jackson, G. A. "Financial Aid and Student Enrollment." *Journal of Higher Education, 49,* 1978, 548–574.

Kreutner, L., and Godfrey, E.S. "Enrollment Management: A New Vehicle for Institutional Renewal." *College Board Review,* Fall-Winter 1981, pp. 6–9, 29.

Leslie, L. L., and Brinkman, P. T. "Student Price-Response in Higher Education." *Journal of Higher Education,* 1987, *58,* 181–204.

McPherson, M. S., and Schapiro, M. O. *Keeping College Affordable: Government and Educational Opportunity.* Washington, D.C.: Brookings Institution, 1991.

McPherson, M. S., and Schapiro, M. O. *The Student Aid Game: Meeting Need and Rewarding Talent in American Higher Education.* Princeton, N.J.: Princeton University Press, 1998.

Muston, R. *Marketing and Enrollment Management in State Universities.* Iowa City, Iowa: American College Testing Program, 1985.

Paulsen, M. *College Choice: Understanding Student Enrollment Behavior.* Washington, D.C.: George Washington University, 1990.

Rudolph, F. *The American College and University: A History.* Athens: University of Georgia Press, 1990.

St. John, E. P. "Price Response in Enrollment Decisions: An Analysis of High School and Beyond Sophomore Cohort." *Research in Higher Education,* 1990, *31,* 161–176.

Tierney, M. L. "Student Matriculation Decisions and Financial Aid." *Review of Higher Education,* 1980, *3* (2), 14–25.

Tinto, V. *Leaving College: Rethinking the Causes and Cures of Student Attrition.* Chicago: University of Chicago Press, 1987.

DON HOSSLER is professor of educational leadership and policy studies and vice-chancellor of enrollment services at Indiana University, Bloomington. His research interests include college choice, the economics of higher education, and financial aid policy.

7

This chapter provides an annotated list of books, articles, newsletters, and Web sites that will prove helpful to new and experienced administrators. Some of the resources address financial aid and enrollment management from historical and structural perspectives. Many explain how financial aid and enrollment management function in tandem to maintain healthy, accessible institutions.

Recommended Reading

Marie T. Saddlemire

Enrollment Management—Foundations

Dixon, R. (ed.). *Making Enrollment Management Work.* New Directions for Student Services, no. 71. San Francisco: Jossey-Bass, 1995.
Readers who are seeking an explanation of enrollment management should consult the first chapter of this volume, which was written by Dixon. This piece outlines the history of enrollment management and offers examples of structural models for successful administration. The rest of the book provides information about incorporating admissions, financial aid, fiscal and human resources, and technology into the overall enrollment plan.

Hossler, D. *Enrollment Management: An Integrated Approach.* New York: College Entrance Examination Board, 1984.
In the 1980s, as enrollment issues were becoming a priority, Hossler provided this primer for university administrators. This book remains an important resource because it takes the reader back to the basics by describing the theoretical and philosophical foundation upon which enrollment management was built.

Enrollment Management—Structures and Strategies

Dennis, M. J. *A Practical Guide to Enrollment and Retention Management in Higher Education.* Westport, Conn.: Bergin & Garvey, 1998.
This is an effective reference book for administrators who are overseeing or coordinating enrollment management efforts. Based on the premise that

enrollment and retention management are inseparable, the author provides useful advice for engaging the expertise of some unlikely departments to advance institutional goals. Extensive checklists are provided for use during campuswide evaluation and implementation. The book also includes a full chapter on the role of financial aid in enrollment management.

De Cristoforo, J. "The Key Role of the Registrar's Office in Planning and Implementing Enrollment Management Activities." *College and University,* 1996, 72 (1), 14–18.
This article emphasizes the importance of technological advances and special services that allow the registrar to meet the needs of prospective and enrolled students, as well as graduates. Best practices are shared throughout the piece, including ideas for self-registration by computer and "continuous registration" programs that allow for more extensive advising.

Huddleston, T., Jr., and Rumbough, L. P. "Evaluating the Enrollment Management Organization." *College and University,* 1997, 72 (4), 2–5.
This article describes how 226 four-year college and university presidents responded to the Enrollment Management Organizational Survey. The primary purpose of the research was to determine how enrollment management was being implemented on both public and private campuses. Researchers also examined the benefits gained from structural changes, and the level of satisfaction with those changes. Huddleston and Rumbough found a significant difference between the reporting structures of public and private institutions. For the most part, administrators were satisfied with their institutions' enrollment management structures, and find them to be meeting their expectations.

Layzell, D. T. (ed.). *Forecasting and Managing Enrollment and Revenue: An Overview of Current Trends, Issues, and Methods.* New Directions for Institutional Research, no. 93. San Francisco: Jossey-Bass, 1997.
This volume provides information about understanding trends and making projections. Two chapters are dedicated to forecasting methods. The recommended enrollment forecasting techniques combine quantitative and qualitative methodology, and include descriptions of curve-fitting techniques, causal models, and the Delphi process. Details of the revenue projection process are divided into sections by revenue source, and address the unique concerns of both private and public administrators.

Financial Aid—Research and Trends

American Association of State Colleges and Universities. *College Costs and Student Financial Aid, 1989–90 to 1997–98: A Guide to Recent Trends in Student Charges and Financial Aid at Four-Year Public Colleges and Universities.* Wash-

ington, D.C.: American Association of State Colleges and Universities, 1998.
This report indicates that the cost of four-year public colleges and universities is steadily rising and examines the reasons behind tuition and fee increases. The appendix lists selected charges for undergraduates at AASCU colleges and universities for the academic year 1997–1998.

Davis, J. S. (ed.). *Student Aid Research: A Manual for Financial Aid Administrators.* Washington, D.C.: National Association for Student Financial Aid Administrators, 1997.
This manual was designed to assist both new and experienced administrators to gather, analyze, and interpret financial aid research data. Entire chapters are devoted to national databases, survey construction, and models and simulations. Distribution of research findings is discussed, including advice on how to construct an annual report for the department, set goals for enrollment, and communicate the role of financial aid in institutional planning.

McPherson, M. S., and Schapiro, M. O. *Keeping College Affordable: Government and Educational Opportunity.* Washington, D.C.: Brookings Institution, 1991.
This book provides an in-depth, historical look at the patterns of college costs, financing trends, and enrollment. Special attention is given to the effects of tuition charges and financial aid upon disadvantaged students' enrollment. Recommendations are made for improving access through public policy reform.

McPherson, M. S., and Schapiro, M. O. *The Student Aid Game: Meeting Need and Rewarding Talent in American Higher Education.* Princeton, N.J.: Princeton University Press, 1998.
McPherson and Schapiro continue to interpret the financial aid system and its effects upon public institutions. Following an excellent analysis of the financial hurdles that many colleges and universities must overcome in light of decreasing federal support, the authors offer sound advice about negotiating an ongoing strategic plan.

Enrollment Management and Financial Aid

College Board. *A Report on the College Board Colloquium on College Affordability and Enrollment Challenges.* New York: College Board, 1998.
This brief book aptly crystallizes discussions among 160 professionals who participated in the Third Annual Colloquium on Financial Aid. Discourse is centered on college affordability and cost drivers and their effects on enrollment management, with an emphasis on preparing prospective stu-

dents for rising costs. This summary provides insights into the theories of numerous experts in the field, including Michael McPherson and Morton Schapiro, who delivered the keynote address at the event.

Duffy, E. A., and Goldberg, I. *Crafting a Class: College Admissions and Financial Aid, 1955–1994*. Princeton, N.J.: Princeton University Press, 1998.
The authors of this book spent two years researching the histories of sixteen liberal arts colleges in Ohio and Massachusetts. The first several chapters review the issue of student quality, the admissions process, and enrollment pressures during the 1900s. Then the reader is offered a unique discussion of how the coeducation movement and minority recruitment have affected the social structure of higher education. The last two chapters focus on the history of need-based and merit aid in Ohio and Massachusetts.

Hossler, D., Schmit, J., and Vesper, N. *Going to College: How Social, Economic, and Educational Factors Influence the Decisions Students Make*. Baltimore: Johns Hopkins University Press, 1998.
This book is the result of a longitudinal study conducted from 1986 to 1994 that examined the aspirations and accomplishments of Indiana high school students. Students were tracked through high school and for four years following graduation. Using a combination of surveys and interviews, the study addressed six research questions, including how high school students develop postsecondary educational aspirations and how students find out about and choose a college. The findings indicated that most high school students made decisions about their postsecondary plans before entering their sophomore year. In addition, parents had a strong influence on decision making. Administrators, especially those who shape public policy, will find this resource helpful because the research methodology could easily be adapted for local use.

Russo, J. (ed.). "Special Issue: Enrollment Management and Financial Aid." *Journal of Student Financial Aid*, 1996, 26 (3).
This issue, more than any other, indicates the strong link between financial aid and enrollment management. The final chapter speaks directly to the effect of enrollment planning on financial aid awards.

Russo, J. (ed.). "First of Two Issues on College Pricing Strategies." *Journal of Student Financial Aid*, 1997, 27 (3).

Russo, J. (ed.), "Second of Two Issues on College Pricing Strategies." *Journal of Student Financial Aid*, 1998, 28 (1).
These two volumes address the relationships among college costs, financial aid policy, college choice, and enrollment. Four research studies, two in each volume, are presented. The first article examines the ways that net costs for students may be calculated and articulated to prospective students. The sec-

ond research study focuses on the link between financial aid packages and first-year enrollment decisions at four colleges and universities. The third piece is a case study of the effects of changes in financial policy on persistence at a private university. The final article in this series addresses the relationship between financial aid and college choice.

Russo, J. (ed.). "The Contribution of Financial Aid to Student Persistence." *Journal of Student Financial Aid,* 1998, 28 (3).
This issue of the *Journal of Student Financial Aid* describes how financial aid affects the persistence of undergraduate and graduate students. Findings indicate that financial aid had little direct effect on undergraduate student persistence, although an aid package often allowed low-income students to pursue a degree. Graduate students who received grants or loans, rather than assistantships, were more likely to persist. The journal also includes an article on the results of the 1997 National Student Loan Survey. The authors found that, for most students, the debt was not overwhelming and they felt confident about their ability to repay.

Newsletters and Web Sites

Hossler, D. (ed.). *The Enrollment Management Review.* Evanston, Ill.: College Board Midwestern Regional Office.
This quarterly newsletter, edited by Don Hossler of the Indiana University Center for Postsecondary Research and Planning, began publication in 1984. It is an excellent publication for busy administrators who need access to brief articles on the latest issues in enrollment management. More details about the latest issues can be found on the College Board Online Web site (see below).

Roseneck, R. (ed.). *Recruitment and Retention in Higher Education.* Madison, Wisc.: Magna Publications.
This monthly newsletter has been published by Magna Publications since 1987. The list of editorial advisors and contributing editors includes Dr. Lee Noel and Dr. Randi Levitz, of the Noel/Levitz Centers for Institutional Effectiveness. The newsletter contains articles about recruitment techniques and best practices in enrollment management. It also provides administrators with short reports of enrollment management news from across the nation.

College Board Online, http://www.collegeboard.org
College Board Online is designed to provide administrators with the tools for successful recruitment and retention. College Board cosponsors a number of institutes and workshops, which are publicized at this Web address. Administrators will also find College Board documents, as well as links to related sites. Some of the College Board Online literature may be downloaded for your use.

National   Association   of   Student   Financial   Aid   Administrators,
http://www.nasfaa.org
The National Association for Student Financial Aid Administrators (NAS-
FAA) has an outstanding Web site that allows for timely access to legislative, regulatory, and professional development information. NASFAA
sponsors a variety of conferences and workshops, and produces a wealth of
publications, many of which are available for purchase via computer. NAS-
FAA members have the most extensive access to this site, and information
on registration and membership benefits may be found on the home page.
Members are entitled to view a weekly NASFAA newsletter, as well as financial aid news of the day.

*MARIE T. SADDLEMIRE is pursuing her doctorate in the higher education admin-
istration program at Bowling Green State University.*

INDEX

Access, as goal of financial aid, 1, 10–11, 38

Accountability, 25–26

Admissions: Harvard College's early policy on, 5–6; increasing relationship between financial aid and, 20

Admissions officers, origin of position of, 6, 7

Ahlburg, D. A., 62, 64, 65, 66, 69, 70, 71

Akerhielm, K., 61, 64

Allan, R. G., 40

Ambrosio, T. J., 24

American Association of Colleges, Task Force on General Education, 52

American Association of State Colleges and Universities, 20, 24, 92

Andrieu, S. C., 28, 64, 69

Asker, E. H., 28, 63, 69

Astin, A. W., 11–12, 13, 51, 69

Attrition. *See* Persistence

Baker, T. L., 50

Balanced Budget Act of 1997, 14, 56

Baldridge, J. V., 13, 77, 78

Basic Educational Opportunity Grant (BEOG), 10, 38. *See also* Federal Pell Grant program

Baum, S., 88

Bean, J., 13, 51, 62, 78, 84

Becker, G. S., 62

Berger, J., 61, 64

Bradley University, 12

Braxton, J., 81

Brinkman, P. T., 62, 65, 69, 81

Bronner, E., 23, 28

Brooks, S., 9

Brubacher, J. S., 6, 7, 8

Budgeting: institutional, and financial aid, 66, 72–73; performance, by state governments, 26

Cabrera, A. F., 63, 64, 69

California State University at Long Beach, 12

Campaigne, D. A., 49

Carnegie-Mellon University, 12

Carter, D. F., 71

Castañeda, M. B., 64, 69

Chapman, R. C., 81, 82

"Chivas Regal phenomenon," 38

Choice. *See* College choice

Clements, M., 28

Clotfelter, C., 34

College Board, 1, 14, 21, 22, 24, 35, 93

College Board Online, 95

College choice: college costs and, 80–81; as goal of financial aid, 1, 10–11, 38; impact of financial aid on, 12, 13, 63, 65–68, 80–84; persistence and, 70–71; research on, 12, 13; resources on, 94–95; tax credits and, 67; value as consideration in, 27; work and, 52, 67

College costs: causes of increases in, 37; college choice and, 80–81; distinction between cost and price and, 34–37; perceptions of, 64, 70–71, 80; recommendations on, 44–45; resources on, 93, 94–95; rising, 15, 25–26, 33, 35–37, 48; shifted from government to students, 48–49

College dropouts: effect of loan aid increase on, 49; research on, 11–12. *See also* Persistence

College education: economic benefit of, 48; education on value of, 45

College enrollment. *See* Enrollment

College Scholarship Service (CSS), 8, 13

College selection. *See* College choice

College Work Study program, 1, 9, 54

Colleges: budgeting by, and financial aid, 66, 72–73; encouraging youth to attend, 57; expansion in number of, 6, 7, 8, 10; financial aid used to achieve goals of, 84–87; future financial aid policies of, 30; implied contract between students and, 71–72. *See also* Community colleges; Private colleges; Public colleges

Committee on Economic Development, 66

Community colleges: cooperative education programs of, 54; origin of concept of, 8

Competition: among colleges for students, 15, 26–27; among students for college acceptance, 23

Conlan, T. J., 8

Consumerism, 15–16, 27, 38–39, 42
Coomes, M. D., 1–2, 6, 7, 8, 9
Cooperative education programs, 53–54
Coopersmith, G., 81
Corrallo, S. B., 12
Corrections funding, 24
Corwin, T. M., 12
Costs. *See* College costs
Craft, L. N., 12
Cronin, J. M., 57

Davis, J. A., 12
Davis, J. S., 24, 28, 48, 93
De Bard, R., 2
De Cristoforo, J., 92
Deans of admissions. *See* Admissions officers
Demographic trends, 15, 22–23, 47
Dennis, M. J., 23, 91
Des Jardins, S. L., 62, 63, 64, 65, 66, 69, 70, 71
Discounting: tuition, 23, 87; defined, 39–40; by private colleges, 43–44, 83; by public colleges, 83, 88, 89n1
Dixon, R., 91
Douvan, E., 12
Dresch, S. P., 62
Duffy, E. A., 7, 8, 10, 11, 12, 13, 14, 38, 40, 41, 94

Eaglin, R., 20
Eaton, J. S., 13
Economic class: college costs and, 48; education tax incentives and, 15, 55; persistence and, 70–71; willingness to obtain loans and, 49. *See also* Middle class
Economy, higher education funding and, 24–25
Edgerton, R., 84, 87
Education Resources Institute, 24
Educational Opportunity Act of 1964, 9
Educational Opportunity Grant program, 9
Ehrenberg, R., 51
Elliott, R. J., 62
Employment. *See* Work
Endowments, 39
Enrollment: current, 23; future, 15, 23; GI Bill's effect on, 8; part-time vs. full-time, 47; in sixties through eighties, 10, 12; of students of nontraditional age, 47
Enrollment, first-time. *See* College choice

Enrollment management: administrative unit created for, 20; defining, 13, 78–79; ethical concerns in, 87–88; historical background of, 5–16; origin of term, 12, 77; resources on, 91–92, 93–95
Enrollment Management Organizational Survey, 92
Enrollment managers, 42

"Federal Education Programs," 6
Federal Family Education Loan Program (FFELP), 9, 14. *See also* Guaranteed Student Loan (GSL) program
Federal government: budget surplus of, 25; financial aid assistance from, 49; financial aid legislation of, 7–8, 9, 10–11, 13–15; future financial aid policies of, 29, 30, 44–45; GI Bill of Rights of, 7–8; higher education funding by, 21; land grant legislation of, 6; National Youth Administration (NYA) legislation of, 7
Federal Pell Grant program, 14; choice as goal of, 1, 10, 29, 38; states required to match grants from, 30
Federal Perkins Loan, 1, 8
Financial aid: college choice and, 12, 13, 63, 65–68, 80–84; consumerism and, 15–16, 27, 38–39, 42; federal appropriations for, 21, 49; federal legislation on, 7–8, 9, 10–11, 13–15; future policies on, 27–31; goals of, 10–11, 19–22, 79–80; from institutions, 22, 37, 39–40; leveraging of, 23, 41–42, 83–84, 87; merit-based, 21–22, 29–30, 40–41, 44, 87; need-based, 21, 29; origin of concept of, 5, 16; packaging of, 26–27, 41–42, 66, 86–87; persistence and, 28, 63, 68–72, 84, 95; research on effects of, 61–65; resources on, 93–95, 96; state appropriations for, 21; student financial services approach to, 42–43
Financial aid consultants, 15, 42, 57
Financial aid offices: development of, 7, 8–9; increasing role for, 19–20; student financial services approach of, 42–43
Fishberg, E., 39

Gaining Early Awareness and Readiness for Undergraduate Program (GEAR UP), 30
Geddes, C. M., 6, 7, 10

Georgia Hope Scholarship, 22
GI Bill of Rights, 7–8, 38
Gladieux, L. E., 6, 9, 48, 49
Godfrey, E. S., 13, 77
Godzicki, R. J., 5
Goldberg, I., 7, 8, 10, 11, 12, 13, 14, 38, 40, 41, 94
Gose, B., 42
Grants: block, to states, 29; college choice and, 66–67; decreasing portion of financial aid as, 14, 21, 49; persistence and, 49
Great Society program, 9
Green, K. C., 13, 53, 77, 78
Guaranteed Student Loan (GSL) program, 10, 11. *See also* Federal Family Education Loan Program (FFELP)

Haller, E. J., 51
Hamm, W. E., 66, 67, 68
Hammes, J. F., 51
Hansen, W. L., 62, 66
Harney, J. Y., 54
Harris, S. E., 6
Harvard College, 5–6
Hauptman, A. M., 48, 49, 54
Hauser, R. M., 49
Healy, C. C., 54
Hebel, S., 55
Heller, D. E., 41, 66, 81
Higher Education Act (HEA) of 1965, 9, 13, 38
Higher Education Act (HEA): 1972 Amendments to, 10, 11; 1992 Amendments to, 14, 25; 1998 Amendments to, 30
Hoffman, C. M., 6, 7, 10
Hooker, M., 61, 64
Hope Scholarship program, 14–15, 55–56
Hossler, D., 2, 5, 6, 7, 12, 13, 49, 62, 77, 78, 81, 82, 83, 91, 94, 95
Howard, M. D., 12
Hu, S., 28
Huddleston, T., Jr., 92

Implied contract, between institutions and students, 71–72
Institute for Higher Education Policy, 24
Institutional aid: funding of, 39–40; increase in, 22; as raising college costs, 37
Institutional choice. *See* College choice
IRAs, withdrawals from, for education, 56

Jackson, G. A., 62, 65, 66, 81, 82
Jackson, R., 81, 82
Jenkins, R. E., 40
Johnson, L. B., 9

Kane, T. J., 15, 48, 62, 63
Katz, J., 52
Kaye, C., 12
Kemerer, F. R., 13, 77, 78
Kent, L., 12
King, J., 51, 54
Kirshstein, R. J., 28, 69
Knapp, L. G., 48, 49
Knight, S., 55, 56
Koff, R. H., 54
Kreutner, L., 13, 77
Kurz, K. A., 49, 57

La Guardia Community College, 54
Lackey, C. W., 42
Laird, T.F.N., 41
Lane County Community College, 54
Lange, M. L., 9
Lapovsky, L., 22
Layzell, D. T., 92
Lederman, D., 55, 56
Leslie, L. L., 62, 65, 69, 81
Leveraging, financial aid, 23, 41–42, 83–84, 87
Levitz, R., 95
Lifetime Learning Credits program, 14–15, 55–56
Linsley, C. B., 54
Loans: college choice and, 67; increasing college costs and, 37; as increasing portion of financial aid, 14, 21, 49; lower-income students' reluctance to obtain, 49; for part-time vs. full-time students, 50; persistence and, 49, 69–70, 71–72. *See also specific loan programs*
Loans. *See* Student loans
Lovett, C. M., 53
Lynton, E. A., 55

Maguire, J., 77
Major beadle, 6
Manski, C. F., 63, 65, 66
McCall, B. P., 62, 64, 65, 66, 69, 70, 71
McCartan, A. M., 51, 52, 53
McGuire, J., 12
McKeown-Moak, M. P., 21, 22, 25, 26
McPherson, M. S., 16, 20, 24, 27, 28, 29, 39, 40, 48, 49, 66, 67, 73n2, 80, 87, 88, 93, 94

Merisotis, J. P., 49, 54, 55, 56
Merit-based scholarships: enrollment management as purpose of, 40–41; increasing number of, 21–22, 29–30, 87; research on effect of, 44
Metzner, B., 13, 51
Middle class: financial aid broadened to benefit, 10–11; tuition tax credits and, 15, 55. See also Economic class
Middle Income Student Assistance Act (MISAA), 11
Mingle, J., 54
Minority students, 49, 71
Monro, J., 8
Morrill Acts, 6
Mortenson, T., 30
Mourton, D. L., 54
Mowlson, Lady A. R., 5, 16
Mumper, M., 24, 42
Muston, R., 77, 78

Nakata, Y. F., 50
National Association of State Budget Officers, 24
National Association of State Student Grant and Aid Programs, 21, 22
National Association of Student Financial Affairs Officers, 49
National Association of Student Financial Aid Administrators (NASFAA), 9, 28, 96
National Center for Education Statistics, 47, 48, 50, 51, 54, 55
National Commission on the Cost of Higher Education, 15, 25–26, 34, 37
National Defense Education Act (NDEA), 8, 38
National Defense Student Loan (NDSL) program, 1, 8
National Early Intervention and Scholarship Program (NEISP), 30
National Postsecondary Student Aid Study, 35–37
National Student Aid Council, 9
National Youth Administration (NYA), 7
Need-based aid, 21, 29
Needs analysis: congressional involvement in, 13–14; origin of, 8; revision of methodology for, 44–45
Net price, 34–37, 62–63
Noel, L., 95
Noell, J., 28, 66, 69
Nora, A., 63, 64, 69

Northwestern University, 12
Noya, R., 42

Oescher, J., 28, 64, 69
Orfield, G., 48, 50, 55
Ort, S. A., 2

Packaging: financial aid, 26–27, 86–87; institutional budgeting and, 66; strategies for, 41–42
Parker, T. D., 49
Pascarella, E. T., 13, 51
Patterson, S., 54
Paulsen, M. B., 52, 63, 64, 69, 70, 71, 81
Pell Grants. See Federal Pell Grant program
Perkins Loan program, 1, 8
Persistence: college choice and, 70–71; financial aid and, 28, 63, 68–72, 84, 95; full-vs. part-time attendance and, 50–51; loans and, 49, 69–70, 71–72; research on, 11–12, 13, 28; resources on, 95; work and, 51
Phinney, D., 24
President's Commission on Higher Education, 8
Price: college choice and, 65–66; distinction between cost and, 34; net, 34–37, 62–63; sticker, 34, 35, 37
Prison funding, 24
Private colleges: cost vs. price issue for, 34–37; discounting by, 43–44, 83; financial aid packaging by, 41–42, 44; financial services approach of, 42–43; future issues for, 43–44; goals for, 38–39; increase in cost of attending, 35–37, 48; merit awards by, 40–41
Private sector, college funding and, 45
Productivity, 25–26
Public colleges: discounting by, 83, 88, 89n1; future issues for, 43–44; increase in cost of attending, 35–37, 48
Pugh, S. L., 42

Quality, of private colleges, 38–39

Ramsay, W., 53
Reagan, R., 13
Redd, K., 19, 21, 22, 27
Reindl, T., 19, 21, 22, 27
Research: on college choice, 12, 13; future, 28; on impact of financial aid,

61–65; on merit aid, 44; on persistence, 11–12, 13, 28
Riggs, H. E., 40, 41
"Robin Hood" strategy, 81
Roseneck, R., 95
Rothman, M. L., 66, 67, 68
Rudolph, F., 7, 80
Rudy, W., 6, 7, 8
Rumbough, L. P., 92
Russo, J., 2, 94, 95

Saddlemire, M. R., 2
St. John, E. P., 2, 28, 48, 49, 52, 62, 63, 64, 65, 66, 67, 68, 69, 70, 71, 73n1, 81
Sanford, N., 11
Sanford, T., 31
Savings incentives, 56
Saxton, J., 55, 56
Scannell, J., 53
Schapiro, M. O., 16, 20, 24, 27, 28, 29, 39, 40, 48, 49, 66, 67, 73n2, 80, 87, 88, 93, 94
Schiraldi, V., 24
Schmit, J., 82, 94
Scholarships: merit-based, 21–22, 29–30, 40–41, 44, 87; origin of concept of, 5, 16
Schuh, J. H., 41
Series EE savings bonds, 56
Serviceman's Readjustment Act (GI Bill), 7–8, 38
Sherman, D., 51
Simpson, K., 53
Smith College, 7
Snyder, T. D., 6, 7, 10
Social forces, state education policies and, 23–24
Somers, P., 41, 64, 65, 66, 67, 68
Somers, P. A., 28
Spencer, A. C., 15
Spiegler, M., 27
Stanton, M., 54
Starkey, J. B., 28, 63, 64, 69, 70
State Budget and Tax News, 25
State governments: conditions affecting policies of, 22–25; future financial aid policies of, 29–30, 44; higher education environment defined by, 20–21; higher education funding by, 21–22, 24, 25; prison appropriations by, 24
State Student Incentive Grant Program, 79–80
"Statutes of Harvard," 6
Stern, D. S., 50

Sticker price, 34, 35, 37
Student aid. *See* Financial aid
Student financial aid. *See* Financial aid
Student financial services approach, 42–43
Student loans. *See* Loans
Student persistence. *See* Persistence
Students: changing demographics of, 15, 22–23, 47; employment of, 50–55; full-time vs. part-time, 47, 50–51; implied contract between institutions and, 71–72; nonresident, tuition discounting for, 88, 89n1; of nontraditional age, 47
Summerskill, J., 11, 12
Supplemental Educational Opportunity Grants, 1
Survey Ordinance of 1785, 6

Tax credits, 14–15, 55–56, 67
Tax deductions, 55
Taxpayer Relief Act of 1997, 14, 55
Terenzini, P. T., 13, 51
Terkla, D. G., 69
Tierney, M. L., 81
Tinto, V., 11–12, 13, 28, 62, 63, 68–69, 84
Trach, J. S., 54
Trammel, M. L., 63, 65, 68
Truman Commission, 8
Truman, H., 8
Tuition: discounting of, 23, 39–40, 43–44, 83, 87, 88, 89n1; future policies on, 27–28; increases in, 24, 35–37, 48; public concern about, 25–26; tax credits for, 14–15, 55–56, 67

University of Notre Dame, 43
U.S. Congressional Budget Office, 25
U.S. Department of Commerce, 48
U.S. Department of Education, 14, 61
U.S. General Accounting Office, 24, 37, 49
U.S. National Center for Education Statistics, 21, 23

Value, as factor in college choice, 27
Van Gyn, G., 53
Vaughan, G., 51
Velez, W., 50
Vesper, N., 82, 94
Vogelstein, F., 34

Weathersby, G. B., 62
Weber, J., 28

Weisbrod, B. A., 66
Western Interstate Commission on Higher Education, 22, 23
White, P., 39
Wick, P. G., 44
Wikler, J., 20, 27
William D. Ford Federal Direct Loan program, 14

Wise, D., 61, 64, 65, 66
Wolanin, T. R., 6, 9
Work, 50–55; college choice and, 52, 67; cooperative education programs for, 53–54; extent of, 50–51; linking school and, 52–55; persistence and, 51; work-study programs for, 1, 9, 54

Back Issue/Subscription Order Form

Copy or detach and send to:
Jossey-Bass Inc., Publishers, 350 Sansome Street, San Francisco, CA 94104-1342

Call or fax toll free!
Phone 888-378-2537 6AM-5PM PST; Fax 800-605-2665

Back issues: Please send me the following issues at $23 each
(Important: please include series initials and issue number, such as SS90)

1. SS _____

_____

_____

$ _____ Total for single issues

$ _____ Shipping charges (for single issues *only;* subscriptions are exempt
from shipping charges): Up to $30, add $5^{50} • $30^{01}–$50, add $6^{50}
$50^{01}–$75, add $7^{50} • $75^{01}–$100, add $9 • $100^{01}–$150, add $10
Over $150, call for shipping charge

Subscriptions Please ❏ start ❏ renew my subscription to *New Directions
for Student Services* for the year _____ at the following rate:

❏ Individual $58 ❏ Institutional $104
NOTE: Subscriptions are quarterly, and are for the calendar year only.
Subscriptions begin with the spring issue of the year indicated above.
For shipping outside the U.S., please add $25.

$ _____ Total single issues and subscriptions (CA, IN, NJ, NY, and DC
residents, add sales tax for single issues. NY and DC residents must
include shipping charges when calculating sales tax. NY and Canadian
residents only, add sales tax for subscriptions)

❏ Payment enclosed (U.S. check or money order only)

❏ VISA, MC, AmEx, Discover Card #_____ Exp. date_____

Signature _____ Day phone _____

❏ Bill me (U.S. institutional orders only. Purchase order required)

Purchase order #_____

Name _____

Address _____

_____

_____

Phone_____ E-mail _____

For more information about Jossey-Bass Publishers, visit our Web site at:
www.josseybass.com **PRIORITY CODE = ND1**

OTHER TITLES AVAILABLE IN THE
NEW DIRECTIONS FOR STUDENT SERVICES SERIES
John H. Schuh, Editor-in-Chief
Elizabeth J. Whitt, Associate Editor

SS88   Understanding and Applying Cognitive Development Theory, *Patrick G. Love, Victoria L. Guthrie*

SS87   Creating Successful Partnerships Between Academic and Student Affairs, *John H. Schuh, Elizabeth J. Whitt*

SS86   Beyond Borders: How International Developments Are Changing International Affairs Practice, *Jon C. Dalton*

SS85   Student Affairs Research, Evaluation, and Assessment: Structure and Practice in an Era of Change, *Gary D. Malaney*

SS84   Strategies for Staff Development: Personal and Professional Education in the 21st Century, *William A. Bryan, Robert A. Schwartz*

SS83   Responding to the New Affirmative Action Climate, *Donald D. Gehring*

SS82   Beyond Law and Policy: Reaffirming the Role of Student Affairs, *Diane L. Cooper, James M. Lancaster*

SS81   New Challenges for Greek Letter Organizations: Transforming Fraternities and Sororities into Learning Communities, *Edward G. Whipple*

SS80   Helping African American Men Succeed in College, *Michael J. Cuyjet*

SS79   Serving Students at Metropolitan Universitites: The Unique Opportunities and Challenges, *Larry H. Dietz, Vicky L. Triponey*

SS78   Using Technology to Promote Student Learning: Opportunities for Today and Tomorrow, *Catherine McHugh Engstrom, Kevin W. Kruger*

SS77   Ethics for Today's Campus: New Perspectives on Education, Student Development, and Institutional Management, *Jane Fried*

SS76   Total Quality Management: Applying Its Principles to Student Affairs, *William A. Bryan*

SS75   Contributing to Learning: The Role of Student Affairs, *Steven C. Ender, Fred B. Newton, Richard B. Caple*

SS74   Leveling the Playing Field: Promoting Academic Success for Students of Color, *Irene Harris Johnson, Allen J. Ottens*

SS73   Critical Issues in Judicial Affairs, *Wanda L. Mercer*

SS72   Student Services for the Changing Graduate Student Population, *Anne S. Pruitt-Logan, Paul D. Isaac*

SS71   Making Enrollment Management Work, *Rebecca R. Dixon*

SS70   Budgeting as a Tool for Policy in Student Affairs, *Dudley B. Woodard, Jr.*

SS69   Promoting Student Success in the Community College, *Steven R. Helfgot, Marguerite McGann Culp*

SS67   Successful Drug and Alcohol Prevention Programs, *Eileen V. Coughlin*

SS66   Developing Student Government Leadership, *Melvin C. Terrell, Michael J. Cuyjet*

SS62   The Changing Role of Career Services, *Jack R. Rayman*

SS59   Rights, Freedoms, and Responsibilities of Students, *William A. Bryan, Richard H. Mullendore*

SS57   Effective AIDS Education on Campus, *Richard P. Keeling*

SS48   Designing Campus Activities to Foster a Sense of Community, *Dennis C. Roberts*

SS38   Responding to the Needs of Today's Minority Students, *Doris J. Wright*

SS4   Applying New Developmental Findings, *Lee Knefelkamp, Carole Widick, Clyde A. Parker*